Grammar Practice

Grade 9

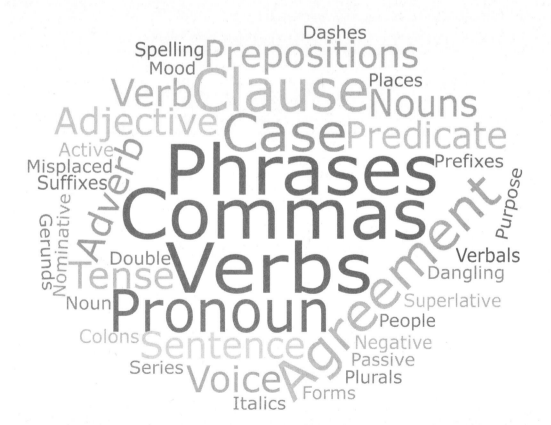

ISBN 978-0-358-26416-3

8 9 10 11 12 0909 28 27 26 25 24 23

4500865304 A B C D E F G

Table of Contents

MODULE 1: THE PARTS OF SPEECH

NOUNS

The Eight Parts of Speech			
noun	adjective	pronoun	conjunction
verb	adverb	preposition	interjection

1a A *noun* is a word used to name a person, a place, a thing, or an idea.

Persons	sister, Uncle Abdul, weaver, friends
Places	house, Malaysia, Milky Way, Detroit
Things	chopsticks, August, Skylab, table
Ideas	love, hate, cooperation, courage

1b A *proper noun* is a word that names a particular person, place, thing, or idea and is always capitalized. A *common noun* is a word that names any one of a group of persons, places, things, or ideas and is not capitalized.

Common Nouns	Proper Nouns
singer	Leontyne Price, Willie Colon
scientist	Leo Esaki, Marie Curie
country	China, Canada
holiday	New Year's Day, Labor Day
school	Dwight Morrow High School

1c A *concrete noun* names an object that can be perceived by the senses. An *abstract noun* names an idea, a feeling, a quality, or a characteristic.

Concrete Nouns	fog, milk, barrel, key, lightning
Abstract Nouns	enthusiasm, pity, ambition, joy

EXERCISE 1   Identifying Common Nouns and Proper Nouns

Underline all of the nouns in the sentences below. If a noun is a proper noun, underline it twice.

EX. 1.   The jogger jumped onto a bus that was going down Broadway.

1.   Dan and his wife Lisa have invented a new way of celebrating Thanksgiving.

2.   The train traveled across Wyoming and into Utah.

3.   China was hit by a severe earthquake on Tuesday.

4.   A cheetah is known for its speed and beauty.

5.   Our new teacher is an expert on jazz.

6.   The doctor knew that measles had caused the blindness.

7.   In the morning, the mat is rolled up and placed in a small closet.

8.   The Great Wall of China is truly an amazing sight!

9.   That haiku was written by Matsuo Bashō.

10.   We read the Declaration of Independence in class.

EXERCISE 2   Identifying Abstract Nouns and Concrete Nouns

In the sentences below, underline the abstract nouns once and the concrete nouns twice.

EX. 1. Our first concert was a success.

1.   Oneida certainly has the talent to become a great painter.

2.   Reverend Ross can discuss all the major religions very well.

3.   On Friday the Sargent Memorial Library will be closed.

4.   Suddenly the screen was filled with pictures of robots.

5.   A variety of dips accompanied the vegetables.

6.   For his report, Jonah read a book about the history of airplanes and locomotives.

7.   People need different kinds of abilities.

8.   Uncle Joe wrote a poem about his dreams.

9.   After the loss, the players showed their disappointment.

10.   The internet might make letter writing a lost art.

COMPOUND NOUNS

1d A *compound noun* consists of two or more words used together as a single noun. The parts of a compound noun may be written as one word. They may also be written as two or more words or as a hyphenated word.

One Word	bodyguard, footprint, newspaper
Two or More Words	high school, Kalahari Desert, League of Nations
Hyphenated Word	great-grandmother, left-hander

NOTE   If you are not sure how to write a compound noun, look it up in a dictionary. Some dictionaries may give two correct forms for a word. For example, you may find the word *vice-president* written both with and without the hyphen. As a rule, use the form your dictionary lists first.

EXERCISE 3   Identifying Compound Nouns

Underline the compound nouns in the sentences below.

EX.   1. The <u>Gateway Arch</u> is a beautiful structure.

1.   At last, Cheng Ho reached the Persian Gulf.

2.   Your bill of sale is proof that you paid.

3.   The nation watched in horror as the spacecraft fell.

4.   The experiment will test how long the night light will burn.

5.   The new cast will be listed on the bulletin board in the hallway.

6.   I'm taking this course so that I can be a lifeguard next summer.

7.   We were supposed to find the icecap on the map.

8.   You can take my sleeping bag when you go fly-fishing.

9.   Do you know how many patents Thomas Alva Edison held?

10.   Some arrowheads were made of flint and some of bone.

MODULE 1: THE PARTS OF SPEECH
REVIEW EXERCISE 1

A.   Identifying Common, Proper, and Compound Nouns

In the paragraph below, underline the common nouns once and the proper nouns twice. Circle the compound nouns. [Note: Some nouns may fit into more than one category.]

EX.   [1] This newspaper stated that <u>Samoyeds</u> are useful <u>animals</u>.

[1] At the beginning of the Space Age, scientists placed a white dog inside *Sputnik II*. [2] The dog, Laika, was a Samoyed, a breed known for its sweet disposition. [3] Samoyeds were originally used by nomadic people in Siberia to herd reindeer and to pull sleds. [4] However, this animal from the former Soviet Union accomplished a new task. [5] Laika became the first living creature to orbit our planet. [6] Laika is also probably the first dog ever to be at an altitude of 1,050 miles above the earth. [7] We do not know exactly why Laika was chosen, but there are three possible reasons. [8] First, its husky build and heavy fur coat allow the Samoyed to stand changes in temperature. [9] Second, the Russians probably wanted a breed of dog from Russia. [10] Third, its strength and intelligence probably helped the Samoyed endure the hardships of the trip.

B.   Classifying Abstract and Concrete Nouns

In the sentences below, underline the abstract nouns once and the concrete nouns twice.

EX. 1.   Do I need <u>talent</u> or <u>luck</u> to become an <u>actor</u>?

1.   My sister and I go to the movies on weekends.

2.   She likes films that are full of romance.

3.   I prefer adventures with characters who show courage.

4.   Is this film about people fighting for their freedom?

5.   The Texans, along with many other people, fought with great bravery at the Alamo.

PRONOUNS

1e A *pronoun* is a word used in place of a noun or more than one noun. This noun, called an *antecedent,* gives the pronoun its meaning.

Personal Pronouns	I, me, my, mine, we, us, our, ours, you, your, yours, he, him, his, she, her, hers, it, its, they, them, their, theirs
Reflexive Pronouns	myself, ourselves, yourself, yourselves, himself, herself, itself, themselves
Indefinite Pronouns	all, another, any, anyone, both, each, everybody, one, everything, few, many, most, no one, some, several

EXAMPLES **Miguel** said that **he** spoke three languages. [*Miguel* is the antecedent of the pronoun *he.*]

Did **Kim** leave **her** wallet on the bus?

Go across the **George Washington Bridge. It** will take you into New York City. [*George Washington Bridge* is the antecedent of the pronoun *It.*]

Notice that a pronoun may appear in the same sentence as its antecedent or in a following sentence.

NOTE Some pronouns, such as possessive forms of pronouns (*my, your,* and *her*) and indefinite pronouns (*all, any,* and *some*) may also be classified as adjectives. Follow your teacher's instructions regarding these forms.

EXERCISE 4   Identifying Pronouns

Underline all the pronouns in the following paragraph.

EX. [1] Kim invited <u>me</u> over to <u>her</u> house.

[1] Kim introduced me to her parents because I had never met them. [2] Kim's father showed me his stamp collection. [3] Each stamp is special because it is not printed anymore or it is from another country. [4] He has stamps from England, Italy, Egypt and many other countries. [5] Some of his stamps have famous people on them. [6] He has a stamp of Charlie Chaplin and one of Booker T. Washington. [7] Washington was the first African

American to get a stamp in his honor. [8] My favorite stamp was the one of John Lennon, my favorite Beatle. [9] Kim's father inspired me to start my own stamp collection. [10] Maybe you would like to start one, too!

EXERCISE 5   Identifying Pronouns and Antecedents

Underline all the pronouns in the following paragraph. On the numbered lines after the paragraph, write the pronouns and their antecedents.

EX. [1] Numerous pirates were men, but not all of them.

1. *them—pirates*

[1] Piracy was common in nineteenth-century China, and not only men were practicing it. [2] A woman named Hsi Kai Ching Yih earned herself a place in history as a famous pirate. [3] Her husband, Ching Yih, was a pirate off the coast of China. [4] Ching Yih married Hsi Kai in 1807 and promised her half of his property. [5] At the time, his property included six squadrons of ships. [6] Ching Yih was lost at sea, and his wife took command of the fleet. [7] At one time, she controlled almost two thousand ships! [8] They were crewed by a total of over fifty thousand pirates. [9] Madame Ching later retired from her adventures at sea. [10] The emperor of China wanted peace, so he gave her a position of honor and a palace.

1. _____   6. _____

2. _____   7. _____

3. _____   8. _____

4. _____   9. _____

5. _____   10. _____

ADJECTIVES

1f   An *adjective* is a word used to modify a noun or a pronoun.

To *modify* a word means to describe the word or to make its meaning more definite. An adjective modifies a noun or a pronoun by telling *what kind, which one*, or *how many*.

What kind?	**green** leaves, **slow** bus
Which one?	**second** book, **first** one
How many?	**forty** people, **three** tacos

The most frequently used adjectives are *a, an*, and *the*. These words are usually called **articles**. *A* and *an* are **indefinite articles**. They indicate that a noun refers to one of a general group. *A* is used before words beginning with a consonant sound. *An* is used before words beginning with a vowel sound.

EXAMPLES   **A** bell rang.   **An** hour had passed.

The is a **definite article**. It indicates that a noun refers to someone or something in particular.

EXAMPLES   **The** bell rang. **The** hour had passed.

An adjective usually comes before the noun or pronoun it modifies. In some cases, adjectives follow the words they modify. Sometimes, other words separate an adjective from the noun or pronoun that it modifies.

EXAMPLES   The **blue** water attracted us. [adjective comes before noun]

The water, **blue** and **cool**, attracted us. [adjectives follow noun]

The water felt **cool**. [word separates adjective from noun]

EXERCISE 6   Identifying Adjectives

Underline each adjective in the following sentences. Do not include definite or indefinite articles.

EX. 1. A <u>magnificent</u> statue stood in the <u>empty</u> hall.

1. Paul saw many medieval manuscripts in the local museum.

2. One manuscript, old and torn, was about a legendary hero.

3. Rodrigo was young, strong, and handsome.

4. He liked fast horses and vigorous activities, including fencing.

5. He became a fierce warrior and a great leader.

6. He fought many long battles in distant countries.

7. In four battles, he carried a jeweled, gleaming sword.

8. Years later, at a splendid ceremony, he became a knight.

9. Proud Rodrigo welcomed relatives and old friends to the ceremony.

10. Knights in colorful clothing and ladies in elegant dresses applauded.

EXERCISE 7   Revising Sentences by Supplying Adjectives

Supply adjectives for the sentences below. Write the adjectives on the lines in the sentences.

EX. 1. Matsu lived in a _____*large*_____ apartment building.

1. Down the street was a _____ shopping center.

2. One store had _____ clothes.

3. Another store looked _____ .

4. The _____ bus stopped for me.

5. At dawn the streets were _____ and _____ .

6. Our _____ steps are _____ , so be careful.

7. _____ people stood impatiently beside the _____ sign.

8. Who gave us _____ tickets?

9. You need a _____ jacket and tie for this job.

10. The crowd at the stadium sounded _____ and _____ .

MODULE 1: THE PARTS OF SPEECH

PRONOUNS AND NOUNS USED AS ADJECTIVES

1g **Some words may be used as either pronouns or adjectives. When used as pronouns, these words take the place of nouns. When used as adjectives, they modify nouns.**

Pronoun	Adjective
Take **this**.	Use **this** brush.
Neither is home.	**Neither** person is home.

The words *mine, my, your, yours, his, her, hers, its, our, ours, their*, and *theirs* are called pronouns in this book. They are the **possessive** forms of personal pronouns, showing ownership or relationship. Some teachers prefer to call such words adjectives because the words tell *which one* about nouns: *my* radio, *your* ticket. Follow your teacher's instructions in labeling such words.

When a noun is used as an adjective, your teacher may prefer that you call it an adjective. Proper nouns used as adjectives are called **proper adjectives**.

1h **Some words may be used as either nouns or adjectives.**

COMMON NOUNS	**autumn**	**water**
ADJECTIVES	**autumn** leaves	**water** safety
PROPER NOUNS	**New York**	**Navajo**
ADJECTIVES	**New York** bank	**Navajo** blanket

EXERCISE 8   Identifying Nouns, Pronouns, and Adjectives

Identify each italicized word in the following sentences. Write *n.* for *noun, pron.* for *pronoun*, or *adj.* for *adjective* on the line before each sentence.

EX. ____*adj.*____   1. Mario gave his mother an *electric* wok.

_____   1. Her birthday is *next* week.

_____   2. Mrs. Vargas said that woks are very *useful*.

_____   3. Only *some* are electric.

_____   4. Most woks need a separate *heat* source.

_____   5. Now she is cooking summer dishes, such as celery *salad*.

_____   6. That recipe came from a *Chinese* cookbook.

_____   7. Soon she will make heartier dishes for *winter*.

_____ 8. *That* is my favorite time of year.

_____ 9. Maybe she will make *that* duck dish we like.

_____ 10. I think it's called *Shanghai* duck.

_____ 11. Did Hideko bring the *cheese* sandwiches or the chips?

_____ 12. Kevin and I need *some* help, Ms. Thompson.

_____ 13. Dr. Kostas is traveling to *Chicago* next Wednesday.

_____ 14. The weather report warned *Texas* residents about a possible hurricane.

_____ 15. Do you like *that*?

_____ 16. *Either* person could work at the concession stand.

_____ 17. The *bitter* cold caused several pipes to freeze.

_____ 18. *Summer* is my favorite time of year.

_____ 19. *Neither* looks good enough to eat.

_____ 20. The *Thanksgiving* choir program was a success.

EXERCISE 9   Revising Sentences by Using Appropriate Adjectives

For each sentence below, add at least one common or proper noun used as an adjective. Write your revised sentences on your own paper.

EX. 1. The cat approached the woman.

1. The Siamese cat approached the young woman.

1. The house was built on a road near me.

2. Trucks rumbled past the store on the corner.

3. A clerk helped me find a sweater.

4. Becky gave a speech in front of the students.

5. On the dresser lay a box.

REVIEW EXERCISE 2

A. Identifying Nouns, Pronouns, and Adjectives

In each of the sentences below, tell how the italicized word is used. Write *comm.* for *common noun, prop.* for *proper noun, comp.* for *compound noun, pron.* for *pronoun,* or *adj.* for *adjective.* [Note: Some nouns may fit into more than one category.]

    EX. *comm.* 1. This *ticket* is yours.

_____ 1. You can almost feel the *excitement!*

_____ 2. *Everyone* is waiting to board the submarine.

_____ 3. Is it a *nuclear* submarine?

_____ 4. This ship can stay underwater for *weeks!*

_____ 5. Didn't *Ferdinand Magellan* travel on this route?

_____ 6. This submarine took *twelve* weeks for its journey.

_____ 7. *This* must be as long as a football field!

_____ 8. The galley, *small* but complete, is below the control room.

_____ 9. This ship even has a *recreation room* on it.

_____ 10. I've never seen *anything* like it.

B. Identifying Abstract and Concrete Nouns

In each of the sentences below, underline the abstract nouns once and the concrete nouns twice.

    EX. 1. A <u>day</u> in the <u>mountains</u> could end your <u>troubles</u>.

1. "Are you ready?" Joe asked Eddie, with excitement in his voice.

2. "Don't we need food and water for the trip?" asked Eddie.

3. Eddie hid his fear when he saw the gigantic mountain.

4. They climbed the mountain with great determination.

5. Because Joe had always wanted to be a mountain climber, his enthusiasm was great.

6. When they reached the top, their spirits soared.

7. As soon as they returned, their mother sighed with relief.

8. "It's an honor to know such brave young men," said their neighbor, Sam.

9. Their classmates looked at them with admiration.

10. Joe sat on the front porch and enjoyed his sudden fame.

C. Identifying Nouns, Pronouns, and Adjectives

Underline each noun, pronoun, and adjective in the sentences below. Do not include *a, an*, and *the*. In the space above each word, write *n.* for *noun, pron.* for *pronoun*, or *adj.* for *adjective*.

        pron.   *adj.*   *n.*

EX. 1. <u>This</u> has been a <u>wonderful</u> <u>day.</u>

1. A bad storm is headed this way.

2. Summer storms can be powerful.

3. Are those clouds getting darker?

4. Everything will get wet if I don't cover it.

5. Did you see that rainbow in the sky?

6. Tropical rains can last a long time.

7. They come during the rainy season in certain parts of the world.

8. He told me people run for cover when they see the storms.

9. Can the hard-working men and women rebuild their homes?

10. We have always prepared for big storms.

D. Working Cooperatively to Write an Advertisement

Working with a partner, create an advertisement to describe and sell a new invention that will help students in school.

1. First, think of what the invention would do and what it might look like. Make your advertisement brief, clear, and interesting. Focus on the most important features of your product, and describe what the product does.

2. Write your advertisement on your own paper. Use at least three nouns and three adjectives in your advertisement. Then underline and label them.

         adj.   *n.*   *adj.*   *n.*

EX. End <u>bookshelf</u> <u>clutter</u> forever! The <u>amazing</u> <u>Presso Paperweight</u>

             adj.   *n.*   *n.*   *n.*

will compress <u>huge</u> <u>piles</u> of <u>paper.</u> Buy <u>Presso Paperweight!</u>

MODULE 1: THE PARTS OF SPEECH
VERBS

1i   A *verb* is a word used to express an action or a state of being.

Words such as *do, come, go,* and *write* are **action verbs.** Sometimes action verbs express actions that cannot be seen: *believe, understand, love.*

A *transitive verb* is an action verb that expresses an action directed toward a person or thing named in the sentence.

EXAMPLES   Lorie **welcomed** the visitors to the game. [The action of the verb *welcomed* is directed toward *visitors*.]

Juan **served** the bread and the herb butter. [The action of the verb *served* is directed toward *bread* and *butter*.]

The action expressed by a transitive verb passes from the doer—the subject—to the receiver of the action. Words that receive the action of a transitive verb are called *objects*.

An *intransitive verb* expresses action (or tells something about the subject) without passing the action from a subject to an object.

EXAMPLES   A cold wind **blew** over the tundra.
We **rode** in silence.

A verb may be transitive in one sentence and intransitive in another.

EXAMPLES   Liang **left** his book. [transitive]
Liang **left** early. [intransitive]

EXERCISE 10   Identifying Action Verbs

In each of the following sentences, underline the action verb once. If the verb is transitive, underline its object twice.

EX.   1. Tom <u>conducted</u> an <u>experiment</u> in his kitchen.

1. In science class, Mrs. Velade discussed chemical reactions.
2. She provided glasses and various liquids.
3. Tom filled a glass with water.
4. He stirred soda into the water.
5. Another student found a bottle of vinegar nearby.
6. Rosa poured some vinegar into a second glass.

7. No one noticed anything special about the mixtures.

8. Then Tom poured the vinegar into the soda solution.

9. Many small bubbles suddenly rose to the surface.

10. The reaction between the two different liquids created a gas.

EXERCISE 11   Identifying Transitive and Intransitive Verbs

Underline the verb in each sentence below. On the line before the sentence, write *trans.* if the verb is transitive or *intr.* if it is intransitive.

EX. _____   1. My train tickets <u>arrived</u> today.

_____   1. Many families waited at the station.

_____   2. Two men boarded the train ahead of me.

_____   3. Haruo read my travel plans very carefully.

_____   4. The train moved quickly along the smooth track.

_____   5. A woman sold food to the hungry passengers.

_____   6. After lunch, I slept for about an hour.

_____   7. The train reached the station at exactly three o'clock.

_____   8. We studied the subway maps on the wall.

_____   9. Our visit to Boston ended too soon.

_____   10. We took the same train home on Sunday afternoon.

EXERCISE 12   Using Transitive and Intransitive Verbs

Choose five verbs from the list below. On your own paper, use each verb in two sentences. The verb should be transitive in one sentence and intransitive in the other. After each sentence, label the verb *intr.* for *intransitive* or *trans.* for *transitive*.

ate	answered	flew
read	remember	cheered
study	watched	struck

EX. 1. *I ate after she did.* (*intr.*)

Danielle ate her salad. (*trans.*)

LINKING VERBS

1j A *linking verb* serves as a link between two words. The most commonly used linking verbs are forms of the verb *be.*

Forms of *Be*			
am	can be	will be	may have been
are	could be	would be	might have been
is	may be	have been	shall have been
was	might be	has been	should have been
were	shall be	had been	will have been
being	should be	could have been	would have been

Here are some other frequently used linking verbs.

Other Linking Verbs			
appear	grow	seem	stay
become	look	smell	taste
feel	remain	sound	turn

The noun, pronoun, or adjective that follows a linking verb completes the meaning of the verb and refers to the noun or pronoun that comes before the verb.

EXAMPLES   The writer **is** Sandra Cisneros. [writer = Sandra Cisneros]
                  The writer **is** talented. [talented writer]

Many linking verbs can be used as action (nonlinking) verbs as well.

EXAMPLES   Roger **felt** happy this morning. [linking verb—happy Roger]
                  Roger **felt** the rough fabric. [action verb—object *fabric*]

Even *be* is not always a linking verb. It is sometimes followed by only an adverb.

EXAMPLES   They are **inside.**

To be a linking verb, the verb must be followed by a noun or a pronoun that names the subject, or by an adjective that describes the subject.

EXERCISE 13   Identifying Linking Verbs and the Words They Link

In each of the sentences below, underline the linking verb once. Draw two lines under the words that are linked by the verb.

EX. 1. <u>Sue Ann</u> <u>seems</u> <u>interested</u> in horses.

1. This ranch in Wyoming is a camp for riders.

2. The riders appeared calm during the show.

3. The campers felt tired after a long day on the trail.

4. The horses are probably hungry and thirsty by now.

5. When the sky grew dark, the campers went into their tents.

6. The pack horses should be ready by now.

7. Food from an open fire tastes wonderful!

8. Even after a day of riding, everyone remained cheerful.

9. I felt sore only on the first day, Friday.

10. Soon the boys and girls were comfortable outdoors.

EXERCISE 14   Writing Appropriate Linking Verbs

On the line in each sentence below, write a linking verb. Use a different verb for each sentence. You may use the verbs from the boxes at the beginning of section 2j.

EX. 1. The sky _____*looked*_____ threatening.

1. The storm _____ scary.

2. That thunder _____ so loud!

3. Nadim _____ nervous as the storm approached.

4. The air _____ moist and heavy.

5. That lightning _____ very close now.

6. You and I _____ safe inside the house.

7. The electricity _____ off for only a few minutes.

8. Severe storms _____ dangerous.

9. The air _____ cool after the rain.

10. The grass _____ wet for a long time.

VERB PHRASES

1k A *verb phrase* consists of a main verb preceded by at least one *helping verb* (also called an *auxiliary verb*). Besides all forms of the verb *be,* helping verbs include

can	do	has	might	should
could	does	have	must	will
did	had	may	shall	would

Notice how helping verbs work together with main verbs to make a verb phrase.

EXAMPLES **is** leaving   **may** become   **might have** been
had seemed   **should** move   **must have** thought
shall be going   **could** jump   **does** sing

Sometimes the parts of a verb phrase are interrupted by other parts of speech.

EXAMPLES **Did** you **finish** your history paper?
You **could** always **stay** at my house.

NOTE   The word *not* is always an adverb. It is never part of a verb phrase, even when it is joined to a verb as the contraction *–n't.*

EXAMPLES   We **would** not **have left** by that time.
We **would**n't **have left** by that time.

EXERCISE 15   Identifying Verbs and Verb Phrases

Underline the verbs and verb phrases in the following sentences. [Hint: The parts of a verb phrase may be separated by other words.]

EX. 1.   Our plane <u>should arrive</u> around 2:00 P.M.

1. We will not be staying in Richmond Friday.

2. People in Indiana are always talking about basketball!

3. Well, you should see the trophies at Indiana University.

4. The state has long been known for its basketball teams.

5. My sister's team could be playing in the semifinals this year.

6. Did you watch the game last night on Channel 5?

7. The game must not have started on time.

8. Well, the team might not have arrived on schedule.

9. Has everyone visited the Basketball Hall of Fame?

10. That building should have been built in Indiana instead of Massachusetts.

11. Do basketball players from Indiana ever become members of professional teams?

12. I haven't been practicing my jump shot.

13. My uncle has never enjoyed contact sports.

14. An interview with a professional team might be exciting.

15. A lot of people from Indiana must really like basketball.

16. The game of basketball was invented in 1891.

17. Wasn't the game developed by a physical education instructor?

18. The new game was played with a soccer ball and two peach baskets.

19. Didn't the first basketball team have nine players?

20. Originally, only one or two players on the team could shoot the ball.

EXERCISE 16 Writing Verb Phrases

Complete each sentence below by creating a verb phrase that uses the verb in parentheses. Write the verb phrases on your own paper.

EX. 1. I (*shop*) for a birthday present for my brother.

1. *have been shopping*

1. My brother (*take*) an English course.

2. Betty (*finish*) a book in an evening.

3. For her birthday, I (*give*) Sally a special photograph.

4. I (*look*) for a good science fiction story.

5. He (*enjoy*) one of those!

6. The teacher (*talk*) to the parent committee.

7. We (*watch*) a film of last week's game.

8. Who (*won*) the Pulitzer Prize this year?

9. The Pyrenees Mountains (*locate*) between Spain and France.

10. Toshi never (*see*) this movie.

ADVERBS

1l   **An *adverb* is a word used to modify a verb, an adjective, or another adverb.**

An adverb answers the questions *where, when, how,* or *to what extent* (*how long* or *how much*).

Where?	Let's go **inside.** Will you stand **there**?
When?	We can leave **now**! The rain will stop **soon**.
How?	The alarm rang **wildly**. Speak **slowly**.
To what extent?	She **hardly** noticed. The path is **quite** steep.

Adverbs may come before or after the verbs they modify. Sometimes adverbs interrupt parts of a verb phrase. Adverbs may also introduce questions.

EXAMPLES   **Recently** we learned about a new law. [The adverb *recently* modifies the verb *learned*, telling *when* we learned.]

How can we **quickly** climb the rope? [The adverb *how* introduces the question and modifies the verb phrase *can climb*. The adverb *quickly* interrupts the verb phrase and tells *how* we climbed.]

If you aren't sure whether a word is an adjective or an adverb, ask yourself what it modifies. If a word modifies a noun or a pronoun, it is an adjective. If it modifies a verb, an adjective, or an adverb, it is an adverb.

EXAMPLES   Jogging is part of my **daily** routine. [*Daily* modifies the noun *routine*, telling *which* one. In this sentence, *daily* is used as an adjective.]

I run **daily**. [*Daily* modifies the verb *run*, telling *when*. In this sentence, *daily* is used as an adverb.]

EXERCISE 17   Identifying Adverbs

Underline the adverbs in the sentences below. Then draw an arrow to the word or words that each adverb modifies.

EX.   1.   <u>Recently</u>, little rain has fallen.

1.   Newscasters are now warning us about forest fires.

2.   Forest fires can spread rapidly.

3.   Our scout leader often discusses fire safety.

4.   Scouts in this area listen carefully.

5.   We never burn fires in windy weather.

6.   A gust of wind can quickly spread a small fire.

7.   Soon we will find a safe location.

8.   Mr. Stamos always pours water over his fires.

9.   He stirs the coals thoroughly as he pours.

10.   Then he shovels dirt over the wet ashes.

EXERCISE 18   Revising with Adverb Modifiers

Revise the sentences below by adding one adverb modifier for each italicized word or phrase. Use a different adverb in each item. Write your answers on your own paper.

EX.   1.   *Water* the plants.

    1.   *Water the plants weekly.*

1.   We *ran* to school.

2.   She *wore* a beautiful coat.

3.   Three guitars *were playing* all at once.

4.   Leticia *dances*.

5.   Severe thunderstorms *are expected*.

6.   The rain *fell*.

7.   We *ate* the tasty apples.

8.   Lamont *quotes* his grandfather.

9.   I *studied* for my math test.

10.   The baby *is crying*.

OTHER USES OF ADVERBS

1m   Adverbs that modify adjectives often come before the adjectives.

EXAMPLES   This painting is **almost** complete. [The adverb *almost* modifies the adjective *complete*, telling *how complete.*]

This watch is **exceedingly** accurate. [The adverb *exceedingly* modifies the adjective *accurate*, telling *how accurate.]*

The most frequently used adverbs are *too, so,* and *very.* In fact, these words are often overused. Here are some other choices.

Adverbs That Frequently Modify Adjectives		
completely	especially	quite
dangerously	extremely	rather
definitely	largely	surprisingly
dreadfully	mainly	terribly
entirely	mostly	unusually

EXERCISE 19   Identifying Adverbs That Modify Adjectives

Underline the adverb that modifies an adjective in each sentence below. Draw an arrow to the adjective that the adverb modifies.

EX. 1.   The Owens family was <u>rather</u> poor.

1.   J. C. Owens was quite unhealthy as a child.

2.   His parents were really happy about his running.

3.   Running was amazingly good for the boy's health.

4.   The Owens' Cleveland home was entirely different from their first home.

5.   The boy was too shy to explain that his name was J. C. and not Jesse.

6.   In high school, one coach was especially kind to Jesse.

7.   Coach Riley noticed that the young man was surprisingly fast.

8.   The 1936 Summer Olympics were terribly exciting.

9. Winning four track-and-field gold medals was extremely unusual, so Jesse became a star.

10. Definitely talented, in 1976, Jesse Owens won one of America's highest civilian awards—the Medal of Freedom.

1n   Adverbs can modify other adverbs.

EXAMPLES   Don't eat **too** quickly. [The adverb *too* modifies the adverb *quickly*, telling *to what extent*.]

The water covered the town **almost** completely. [The adverb *almost* modifies the adverb *completely*, telling *to what extent*.]

NOTE   Although many adverbs end in *–ly*, the *–ly* ending does not automatically mean that a word is an adverb. Many adjectives also end in *–ly*: a *daily* prayer, a *silly* cartoon, a *lovely* day. Even though some words do not end in *–ly*, they are often used as adverbs. These words include *now, then, far,* and *already.* To identify a word as an adverb, ask yourself two questions.

- Does this word modify a verb, an adjective, or another adverb?
- Does it tell *when, where, how*, or *to what extent*?

EXERCISE 20   Identifying Adverbs That Modify Other Adverbs

Underline the adverb that modifies other adverbs in each sentence below. Draw an arrow to the other adverbs being modified.

EX.   1.   Cheetahs can move <u>very</u> quickly.

1. A sloth almost never travels on the ground.

2. Those armadillos sleep much more than most animals!

3. A sifaka, a type of lemur, lives almost totally in trees.

4. You will be able to read this book on animals quite quickly.

5. Can red kangaroos jump exceedingly high?

6. Wild turkeys, you know, can run surprisingly fast.

7. Gray parrots talk much better than other birds.

8. A few birds fly so slowly that you might expect them to fall from the sky.

9. One bullfrog jumped quite far during our contest.

10. The tiny bristlemouth fish lives almost everywhere!

PREPOSITIONS

1o A *preposition* is a word used to show the relationship of a noun or a pronoun to some other word in the sentence.

EXAMPLES   We hung the picture **beside** the sofa.

We hung the picture **above** the sofa.

We hung the picture **near** the sofa.

Commonly Used Prepositions				
aboard	because of	by	like	past
above	before	concerning	near	since
according to	below	during	next to	through
across	beneath	except	of	to
against	beside	for	off	toward
along	between	from	on	underneath
around	beyond	in addition to	out	until
as of	but (meaning *except*)	inside	over	upon
at		into	owing to	with

NOTE   Many words in the list above can also be adverbs. To be sure that a word is a preposition, ask whether the word relates a noun or a pronoun following it to a word that comes before it.

EXAMPLES   One person lagged **behind.** [adverb]

One person lagged **behind** the others. [preposition]

EXERCISE 21   Distinguishing Prepositions from Adverbs

On the line before each of the following sentences, write *prep.* if the word in italics is a preposition or *adv.* if the word is an adverb.

EX.   *prep.*   1. This exhibit has many pictures *of* children.

_____   1. The name *on* many pictures is Mary Cassatt's.

_____   2. The sketch for this scene is *beside* the painting.

_____   3. One woman is sipping tea from a tray that is sitting *near* the chair.

_____   4. The other woman is sitting just *beyond* her.

_____   5. Look at the big picture as you go *out*.

_____ 6. Mary Cassatt lived in Paris *for* many years.

_____ 7. Once, she painted a scene of Paris *from* her balcony.

_____ 8. She included her dog, which she loved to have *around*.

_____ 9. The dog has the rails of the balcony to lean *against*.

_____ 10. *According to* a biographer, it was one of the few times she painted a picture of the city.

EXERCISE 22   Revising Sentences by Using Appropriate Prepositions

Revise the following paragraph by writing an appropriate preposition or compound preposition on the line in each sentence.

EX. [1] The shield had a picture of a turtle _____*on*_____ it.

[1] Each summer, Native American people _____ many places gather for powwows. [2] In fact, I went to one _____ Saturday. [3] I stood _____ a Chippewa dancer. [4] He wore a colorful costume and had beaded, leather moccasins _____ his feet. [5] He danced beautifully _____ the regular beat of the drums. [6] My sister learned some traditional dances _____ a powwow. [7] Many Native American people in the Northwest live and work _____ cities. [8] Those who want to keep their traditions alive are sometimes caught _____ two cultures. [9] At the powwows, people dance _____ prizes. [10] Native American culture is remembered and preserved _____ powwows.

CONJUNCTIONS AND INTERJECTIONS

1p   A *conjunction* is a word used to join words or groups of words.

Coordinating conjunctions always connect items of the same kind. They may join single words or groups of words. Coordinating conjunctions include *and, but, for, nor, or, so,* and *yet.*

EXAMPLES   songs **and** lyrics [two nouns.]
                in sickness **or** in health [two prepositional phrases]
                First it rained, **but** the rain stopped quickly. [two complete ideas]

Correlative conjunctions also connect items of the same kind. However, unlike coordinating conjunctions, correlatives are always used in pairs. Correlative conjunctions include *both...and, either...or, neither...nor, not only...but also,* and *whether...or.*

EXAMPLES   **Both** dogs **and** cats make good pets. [two nouns]
                You should set flowers **not only** on the table **but also** in the basket. [two prepositional phrases]
                Either borrow a book **or** buy a magazine. [two complete ideas]

EXERCISE 23   Identifying and Classifying Conjunctions

In the following sentences, underline the coordinating conjunctions once and the correlative conjunctions twice. Some sentences contain more than one conjunction.

EX. 1.   I like most fruits, <u>but</u> I don't like <u>either</u> currants <u>or</u> blueberries.

1.   Most fruits and vegetables are good sources of nutrients.
2.   Milk is high in calcium, but it also can be high in fat.
3.   Both cereals and pasta are rich in B vitamins yet low in fat.
4.   Vitamin C is found not only in oranges, but also in strawberries, green peppers, and tomatoes.
5.   I don't know whether to cook this in oil or bake it in the oven.
6.   Sara wants neither lettuce nor sprouts on her sandwich.
7.   Baked, steamed, or boiled potatoes are low in calories, so don't add butter or sour cream.
8.   To make the sauce, use either a blender or an electric mixer.
9.   Joel is concerned about additives, so he has started reading food labels.
10.   May I have both juice and water with my meal?

1q An *interjection* is a word used to express emotion. It has no grammatical relation to the rest of the sentence.

Since an interjection is unrelated to other words in the sentence, it is set off from the rest of the sentence by an exclamation point or a comma.

EXAMPLES   **Hooray!** We won the game!

Oh, I guess it's okay.

Dinner was good, but, **ugh,** that dessert was awful.

No! Our television picture just disappeared.

EXERCISE 24   Writing Sentences with Interjections

On your own paper, use each of the interjections below to create a sentence.

EX. 1. ouch

1. *Ouch! That branch scratched me!*

1. whoa
2. well
3. yikes
4. aww
5. wow

6. ha
7. yippee
8. shh
9. oh dear
10. phew

MODULE 1: THE PARTS OF SPEECH
MODULE REVIEW

A. Identifying the Parts of Speech

On the line before each sentence, identify the part of speech of the italicized word. Write *n.* for *noun*, *v.* for *verb*, *adv.* for *adverb*, *adj.* for *adjective*, *pron.* for *pronoun*, *conj.* for *conjunction*, *prep.* for *preposition*, or *intj.* for *interjection*.

EX. __*adj.*__ 1. Joseph Haydn composed *many* symphonies.

_____ 1. The composer and musician created 104 symphonies, 84 string quartets, *and* many other works.

_____ 2. Did you know that he was *once* expelled from his school?

_____ 3. At the time, Haydn was attending a *choir school* in Vienna.

_____ 4. The choir *sang* in St. Stephen's Cathedral.

_____ 5. In school, a boy with a pigtail stood *in front of* Hyden.

_____ 6. One day, Haydn cut *it* off.

_____ 7. Haydn was seventeen years *old* at the time.

_____ 8. *Well*, the adults at the school were displeased by this.

_____ 9. Haydn was *no* longer a student at that school.

_____ 10. This event did not *seem* to affect his later life, though.

B. Writing Sentences Using the Same Words as Different Parts of Speech

On your own paper, write two sentences for each of the words below, showing how the word can be used as two different parts of speech. Then label how you used each word.

EX. 1. down
  1. *Jonathan looked down.* (*adv.*)
     He tossed the ball down the hill. (*prep.*)

1. race	6. milk	11. for
2. over	7. dark	12. jump
3. building	8. some	13. both
4. game	9. well	14. kick
5. purple	10. beyond	15. knot

C. Working Cooperatively to Determine Parts of Speech in a Message

You have discovered a letter and a treasure map that have been hidden in an attic for many years. Unfortunately, parts of the letter have crumbled away, leaving numerous holes. Work with a partner to supply a word that makes sense for each hole. Write its part of speech in the space above the line. You may use the following abbreviations: *n.* for *noun, v.* for *verb, pron.* for *pronoun, adj.* for *adjective, adv.* for *adverb, prep.* for *preposition, conj.* for *conjunction,* and *intj.* for *interjection.* [Note: Each part of speech is used at least once. You may wish to read the entire letter before you try to fill in the blanks.]

         adj.

EX. Look for a _____*flat*_____ stone.

My dear [1] _____,

 I buried [2] _____ bars of gold and a hundred pieces of silver. If something

happens to me, I want [3] _____ to have them. Be sure to follow my [4]

_____ exactly, and use the map as a reference. On the map, you will see a [5]

_____ hut. In this hut is a closet. The closet is [6] _____ feet to the

right of the [7] _____. The floor [8] _____ the closet [9]

_____ false. It will lift [10] _____. Dig [11] _____

about three feet and look for a metal ring. Pull it [12] _____ as hard as [13]

_____ can. [14] _____! You have discovered the [15]

_____ box. The box is [16] _____ of gold [17] _____

silver. If you are reading [18] _____, I might be dead. Good luck! One of [19]

_____, at least, will get rich.

            Your [20] _____,

            Lemuel

THE SENTENCE

2a **A *sentence* is a group of words that contains a subject and a verb and expresses a complete thought.**

If a group of words does not express a complete thought, it is a ***fragment,*** or incomplete part, of a sentence.

FRAGMENT   the man in the white coat

SENTENCE   The man in the white coat is my uncle.

FRAGMENT   standing in line

SENTENCE   We were standing in line.

FRAGMENT   before you go to the meeting

SENTENCE   Do you want some lunch before you go to the meeting?

Notice that a sentence always begins with a capital letter and ends with a period, a question mark, or an exclamation point.

EXERCISE 1   Identifying Complete Sentences and Sentence Fragments

On the line before each word group below, write *sent.* if it is a sentence or *frag.* if it is not a sentence. Add correct capitalization and end punctuation to the sentences.

               W

EX. *sent.*   1. ~~w~~ould you like a bowl of soup

_____   1. waiting for your phone call

_____   2. help me carry this huge package

_____   3. after the basketball game was over

_____   4. three of my favorite animals

_____   5. did you finish your science project

_____   6. it doesn't bother me

_____   7. someday if we are fortunate

_____   8. the fastest runner on the whole team

_____   9. there is very little money in the treasury

_____   10. hoping to win a scholarship to college

EXERCISE 2   Revising Fragments to Create Complete Sentences

On your own paper, revise each word group below so that it is a complete sentence. Add modifiers and any other words to make the meaning of your completed sentence clear.

EX. 1. in the center of the room

　　1. *In the center of the room stood a large statue.*

1. standing in the lobby
2. nevertheless, I
3. after the concert
4. out in the driveway
5. the men were
6. climbing to the top of the mountain
7. it often
8. this exciting movie
9. late last night while walking home
10. four students on the bus
11. boardsailing in the California surf
12. in ink on a postcard
13. want to try the shrimp
14. now Heidi
15. feeds her chickens
16. in almost every letter
17. were finding shells on the beach
18. from the two new students
19. must reach the Evlers
20. is one of the most dedicated people
21. to apply for this job
22. adjusting the throttle
23. working on a computer
24. changes in fashions
25. should write or read
26. a serious discussion
27. floating in the pool
28. therefore, we
29. just around the corner
30. wanted the answer

A *run-on sentence* is two or more complete sentences run together as one.

There are two kinds of run-ons. In a *fused sentence,* the sentences have no punctuation at all between them.

RUN-ON	Jeremiah moved here from Israel he is my best friend.
CORRECT	Jeremiah moved here from Israel. He is my best friend.

The second kind of run-on is called a *comma splice.* Two sentences are linked together with only a comma to separate them.

RUN-ON	Jeremiah joined the school orchestra, he plays the violin.
CORRECT	Jeremiah joined the school orchestra. He plays the violin.

To revise run-on sentences, you can always make two separate sentences. But if the two thoughts are related and are equal to one another in importance, you may want to make a *compound sentence.*

RUN-ONS	The Delaware River is in eastern Pennsylvania the Ohio River is in western Pennsylvania. [fused]
	The Delaware River is in eastern Pennsylvania, the Ohio River is in western Pennsylvania. [comma splice]

You can revise a run-on sentence by using one of the following techniques.

1. Use a comma and a coordinating conjunction (such as *and, but,* or *or*).

CORRECTED	The Delaware River is in eastern Pennsylvania, and the Ohio River is in western Pennsylvania.

2. Use a semicolon.

CORRECTED	The Delaware River is in eastern Pennsylvania; the Ohio River is in western Pennsylvania.

3. Use a semicolon and a word such as *therefore, instead, meanwhile, still, also, nevertheless,* or *however.* These words are called *conjunctive adverbs.* Follow a conjunctive adverb with a comma.

CORRECTED	The Delaware River is in eastern Pennsylvania; however, the Ohio River is in western Pennsylvania.

EXERCISE 3   Revising Run-on Sentences

On your own paper, revise each of the run-on sentences below. Follow the directions in parentheses. Be sure to use correct end punctuation.

EX. 1.   Jamyce has worked hard on her report, it isn't finished yet. (Use a comma and a coordinating conjunction.)

   1.   *Jamyce has worked hard on her report, but it isn't finished yet.*

1.   Maria Tallchief was a Native American she became one of the world's most famous ballerinas. (Split into two sentences.)

2.   Reiko Amato designed the cover for our yearbook the design won an award presented by the Houston Arts League. (Use a semicolon.)

3.   Delaware is one of the smallest states, Rhode Island is even smaller. (Use a semicolon and a conjunctive adverb.)

4.   The Andes Mountains are in South America, the Alps are in Europe. (Use a comma and a coordinating conjunction.)

5.   We wanted to attend your dress rehearsal, we had to go to a late session of soccer practice. (Use a semicolon and a conjunctive adverb.)

6.   The sound of the motorcycle woke me up, I still didn't get out of bed. (Use a coordinating conjunction.)

7.   *The Joy Luck Club* by Amy Tan was the book we chose for the book group I am so glad we decided to read it. (Use a comma and a coordinating conjunction.)

8.   The storm moved into the area after lunch we had already found shelter. (Use a semicolon and a conjunctive adverb.)

9.   Did you attend the concert my mom wouldn't let me go on a school night. (Split into two sentences.)

10.   I have always loved animals someday I'd like to be a veterinarian. (Use a comma and a coordinating conjunction.)

SUBJECT AND PREDICATE

2b   **A sentence consists of two parts: the subject and the predicate. The *subject* is the part that names the person or thing spoken about in the rest of the sentence. The *predicate* is the part that says something about the subject.**

The subject may be one word or a group of words. The **complete subject** contains all the words that name the person or thing spoken about in the rest of the sentence. The complete subject may appear at the beginning, in the middle, or at the end of a sentence.

                     cmpl. s.
EXAMPLES   **The woman in the red car** just got a speeding ticket.

                     cmpl. s.
             Did **Phoebe's brother** win the poetry contest?

                        cmpl. s.
             Into the water dove **a brown pelican.**

Like the subject, the predicate may be one word or a group of words. The **complete predicate** contains all the words that say something about the subject. Like the complete subject, the complete predicate can appear in many different places in a sentence.

                       cmpl. pred.
EXAMPLES   The woman in the red car **just got a speeding ticket.**

                    cmpl. pred.
     Did Phoebe's brother **win the poetry contest?**

          cmpl. pred.
     Into the water dove a brown pelican.

EXERCISE 4   Identifying the Complete Subject

Underline the complete subject in each of the following sentences.

    EX. 1. <u>What</u> is the source of your information?

    1. The desert is a great place to take photographs.

    2. In outdoor magazines, readers can often find photographs of magnificent deserts.

    3. Have you ever seen photographs of desert landscapes?

    4. In the desert, strong winds can carve deep ridges in the rocks.

    5. Similarly, those fierce winds blast clouds of flying sand against the rocks.

    6. Sand and dust in the wind leave behind a hard surface of bare rocks.

7. The sand is eventually redeposited elsewhere in the desert, often as sand dunes.

8. Standing in dramatic rows in some desert photographs are huge sand dunes.

9. The dunes are constantly shifting and changing shape because of strong winds.

10. The powdery dunes may be compressed into hard layers of sandstone after many thousands of years.

EXERCISE 5   Writing Complete Predicates

On your own paper, write ten complete sentences by adding a complete predicate to each of the subjects below. Be sure to use correct capitalization and end punctuation in your sentences.

EX. 1. the clerk in that store
   1. *The clerk in that store is extremely helpful.*

1. one of the buildings on our street
2. my favorite poem
3. a popular tourist attraction in our area
4. dinosaurs
5. several people
6. the most interesting books
7. political leaders
8. a good way to get exercise
9. the escalator at the north end of the mall
10. the artist
11. llamas and alpacas
12. a sifaka, a kind of lemur,
13. your best friend
14. a group of sixth-graders
15. my favorite holiday

THE SIMPLE SUBJECT AND SIMPLE PREDICATE

2c   The *simple subject* is the main word or group of words within the complete subject.

EXAMPLE	**The letter from Sharon** is on your desk.
COMPLETE SUBJECT	The letter from Sharon
SIMPLE SUBJECT	letter

EXAMPLE	Did **that mysterious Colonel Potter** return my call?
COMPLETE SUBJECT	that mysterious Colonel Potter
SIMPLE SUBJECT	Colonel Potter

NOTE   In this book, the term *subject* refers to the simple subject unless otherwise indicated.

EXERCISE 6   Identifying Complete Subjects and Simple Subjects

In each sentence below, underline the complete subject once, and draw a second line under the simple subject.

EX. 1. The talented Ansel Adams was a photographer, a conservationist, and a writer.

1. Ansel Adams' photographs of Yosemite Valley are very dramatic.

2. Time after time, Adams filmed the stark beauty of the canyons.

3. His experiments with light and shutter speed made him unique.

4. Many talented photographers have tried to duplicate Adams' work, without success.

5. The photographer wrote in his many books about his photographic techniques.

6. He often photographed mountains, forests, and rivers.

7. Adams' style of photography is called *straight photography.*

8. *Straight photography* shows the subjects of the pictures simply and directly.

9. Adams established photography departments in several schools.

10. One of these departments is at the San Francisco Art Institute.

2d The *simple predicate*, or *verb*, is the main word or group of words within the complete predicate.

EXAMPLE	He **wasn't going to the movie.**
COMPLETE PREDICATE	wasn't going to the movie
SIMPLE PREDICATE	was going
EXAMPLE	**In a little while,** the fireworks **should begin.**
COMPLETE PREDICATE	should begin in a little while
SIMPLE PREDICATE	should begin

The simple predicate may be a single verb or a verb phrase. A **verb phrase** is a main verb and its helping verbs.

EXAMPLES   is walking   has been called   will have seen

When you look for the simple predicate in a sentence, be sure to include all parts of the verb phrase. Keep in mind the various helping verbs, such as *am, is, were, do, have, can, will*, and *could*.

NOTE   In this book, the word *verb* refers to the simple predicate unless otherwise indicated.

EXERCISE 7   Identifying Complete Predicates and Simple Predicates

In each sentence below, underline the complete predicate once, and draw a second line under the simple predicate. Be sure to include all parts of a verb phrase.

EX. 1. Ravi <u>was leading the band at practice yesterday</u>.

1. The high school band has finally gotten new uniforms after many years.
2. They are black with orange stripes down the pant legs and the sleeves.
3. A committee raised the money for the uniforms.
4. They earned almost three thousand dollars through car washes, bake sales, and a flea market.
5. Everyone in the band helped with these activities.
6. The band members will appear in their new uniforms tonight.
7. Dr. Beach has arranged for the appearance of four other high school bands from various parts of the city.
8. All the band members will march into the stadium in uniform.
9. Then they will play the "Star-Spangled Banner" together.
10. Are you going to the concert?

The best way to find the subject of a sentence is to find the verb first. Then ask "Who?" or "What?" in front of it.

EXAMPLES   Each month at the library, you can meet the author of a best-selling novel. [The verb is *can meet. Who* can meet? *You* can meet. *You* is the subject.]
The fuel for the lantern is in the shed. [The verb is *is. What* is in the shed? *Fuel* is in the shed. *Fuel* is the subject.]

2e   The subject of a verb is never in a prepositional phrase.

EXAMPLES   The secretary to the principal is Ms. Gómez. [*Secretary* is the subject. The prepositional phrase *to the principal* modifies the subject.]
The car with the flat tire limped into the service station. [*Car is* the subject. The prepositional phrase *with the flat tire* modifies the subject.]

2f   You can find the subject in a question by turning the question into a statement. Find the verb in the statement and ask "Who?" or "What?" in front of it.

Questions often begin with a verb, a helping verb, or a word such as *what, where, when, how*, or *why*. The subject usually follows the verb or helping verb.

EXAMPLE   Has the plane left? **becomes** The plane has left. [*What* left? The *plane* left.]

2g   Do not mistake the word *there* for the subject of a sentence. To find the subject in this type of sentence, omit *there* and ask "Who?" or "What?" before the verb.

There is often used to get a sentence started when the subject comes after the verb.

EXAMPLE   There are many worms in the compost pile.
[*What* are in the compost pile? The *worms* are. *Worms* is the subject.]

NOTE   Like *there*, the adverb *here* is often used to get a sentence started. To find the subject in such a sentence, omit *here* and ask "Who?" or "What?" before the verb.

    EXAMPLE   Here is your ticket. [*What* is? *Ticket* is. *Ticket* is the subject.]

2h   In a request or a command, the subject of a sentence is usually not stated. In such sentences, *you* is the *understood subject*.

REQUEST   Please feed the cat. [*Who* should feed the cat? *You* should feed the cat. *You* is the understood subject.]

COMMAND   Don't talk during his speech. [*Who* shouldn't talk? *You* shouldn't talk. *You* is the understood subject.]

Sometimes a request or command will include a name. Names used in commands or requests are called **nouns of direct address.** They identify the person spoken to or addressed, but they are not subjects. *You* is still the understood subject.

EXAMPLE   Marie, (you) please deliver this note for me.

EXERCISE 8   Identifying Subjects and Verbs

In the sentences below, underline each subject once. Underline the verb twice. If the understood subject is *you*, write *you* on the line before the sentence.

EX. _____ 1. There <u>are</u> almost forty new <u>houses</u> on this road.

_____ 1. Rodney, return your books to the library.

_____ 2. When will the candidate make a speech here?

_____ 3. Here are the directions to my house.

_____ 4. Take the dog for a walk around the block.

_____ 5. Did your mother enjoy the concert?

_____ 6. There is a new movie at the Fox Theater tonight.

_____ 7. Will you need a ticket to the lecture?

_____ 8. Is Harrisburg the capital of Pennsylvania?

_____ 9. Priscilla, watch the children in the pool.

_____ 10. Be quiet!

_____ 11. Can you play badminton?

_____ 12. The quarterback, along with the coach, left early.

_____ 13. Learn the rules by Wednesday.

_____ 14. Dorothea Dix, with Elizabeth Blackwell, helped the sick.

_____ 15. There was a nail in my shoe.

2i   A *compound subject* consists of two or more subjects that are joined by a conjunction and have the same verb.

The conjunctions most commonly used to connect the words of a compound subject are *and* and *or*.

EXAMPLE   **Lucia** and **Donald** brought refreshments for the team. [*Who* brought refreshments? *Lucia* brought them. *Donald* brought them. *Lucia* and *Donald* form the compound subject.]

When more than two words are included in the compound subject, the conjunction is generally used only between the last two words. Also, the words are separated by commas.

EXAMPLE   Lucia, Donald, **and** Sophia brought refreshments for the team. [Compound subject: *Lucia, Donald, Sophia*]

Correlative conjunctions may be used with compound subjects.

EXAMPLE   **Either** Lucia **or** Donald will bring refreshments for the team. [Compound subject: *Lucia, Donald*]

2j   A *compound verb* consists of two or more verbs that are joined by a conjunction and have the same subject.

EXAMPLES   The photographer **ran** up the aisle and **snapped** the president's picture.
I **listened** to the game on the radio but **missed** the fourth inning.
Our team **won** four games, **lost** two, and **tied** three.
Congress **will** either **approve** the bill or **suggest** some changes.

Notice that in the last sentence, the helping verb *will* is not repeated before the second verb, *suggest*. In compound verbs, the helping verb may or may not be repeated before the second verb if the helper is the same for both verbs.

EXERCISE 9   Identifying Compound Subjects and Their Verbs

In each of the following sentences, underline the compound subject once and the verb twice.

EX.   1.   <u>Birds and lizards</u> <u><u>might be</u></u> modern relatives of dinosaurs.

1.   Either Tanya or Mae Ellen will win the election.

2. There are your shoes and socks, under your bed.

3. Are Helena and Miguel staying for dinner?

4. In the cold waters of this stream, many trout, bass, and pickerel live.

5. At the bottom of the drawer were needles, thread, and even extra buttons.

6. Bottles of juice and cartons of milk were standing in the cooler.

7. Neither my brother nor my sister can come to the concert on Friday.

8. Only Jeremy and I know the location of the buried treasure.

9. Here are Jim and Sandy at the bus stop, right on time.

10. In April, my sisters and I are visiting colleges in Maine and Utah.

EXERCISE 10   Identifying Subjects and Compound Verbs

In each sentence below, underline the subject once and the compound verb twice. Be sure to include any helping verbs.

EX.   1.   They visited Canada but did not go to Banff.

1. The fielder shielded her eyes, saw the ball, and moved quickly to her left.

2. I opened the door but saw no one on the porch.

3. Tomorrow morning we will either go to the beach or walk into town for breakfast at the diner.

4. Odessa will direct the play and perform the role of Lady Macbeth.

5. Ray Charles wrote the music and lyrics for his songs and played the piano extremely well.

6. You can come to Puerto Rico, relax on the beach, and visit our great shops and restaurants.

7. At night you can eat dinner and look out at the Caribbean Sea.

8. The new computers at the library have flat-screen monitors and are available for everyone's use.

9. My cousin joined the Houston Museum of Natural Science last year and has gone to many interesting programs there.

10. Could you meet me right after school today or come to my house after soccer practice?

COMPLEMENTS

2k   A *complement* is a word or group of words that completes the meaning of a predicate.

Notice how the following sentences need the complements to complete the meaning of the predicates. The complement may be a noun, a pronoun, or an adjective, and may be compound. The best way to find the complement in a sentence is to ask who or what receives the action of the verb.

EXAMPLES
         s   v   c
Denzel Washington is a great **actor.** [noun]

           s   v   c
The coach advised **us.** [pronoun]

        s v   c   c
She is always **friendly** and **polite.** [compound adjective]

         s   v   c   c
Dr. Ramírez helped **Velma** and **me.** [noun and pronoun]

NOTE   The complement of a sentence is never part of a prepositional phrase.

        EXAMPLES   She fed the **dog.** [*Dog* is the complement.]

                        She called to the **dog.** [*Dog* is part of the prepositional phrase *to the dog.*]

EXERCISE 11   Identifying Subjects, Verbs, and Complements

In each of the following sentences, underline the simple subject once and the verb twice. Then put brackets around the complement. [Hint: Some sentences may have a compound complement.]

EX. 1. <u>Marie</u> <u>rented</u> an old [movie] last night.

1. Her great-grandfather had recommended the movie to her.
2. Marie enjoys mysteries and courtroom dramas.
3. The name of the movie was *Witness for the Prosecution.*
4. Three very famous actors from Great-Grandpa's era had the leading roles.
5. Charles Laughton, famous as the hunchback in *The Hunchback of Notre Dame*, played the defense attorney in *Witness for the Prosecution.*
6. A very famous actor, Tyrone Power, played the defendant.
7. Marlene Dietrich was one of the most beautiful and most talented women in film history.

8. She played the defendant's wife and the chief witness for the prosecution.

9. Throughout the movie, twists and turns in the plot keep viewers on the edges of their seats.

10. Do not reveal the surprise ending to anyone!

11. We often rent old movies at our house, too.

12. My favorite old movie is *It Happened One Night.*

13. This movie stars Clark Gable and Claudette Colbert.

14. It received the Academy Award for best picture in 1934.

15. The same year, Gable and Colbert each received an Academy Award for best actor and best actress, respectively.

EXERCISE 12 Writing Sentence Complements

Complete the sentences below by adding a complement to each group of words. Add any other words necessary to make your sentences clear.

EX. 1. Tomorrow Penny will give _a speech_ .

1. Gina sometimes seems _____ .

2. Do you need _____ or _____ ?

3. Last Thursday, I finished _____ and _____ .

4. Barbara won _____ .

5. This bread tastes _____ .

6. That painting is really _____ .

7. Could I borrow your _____ ?

8. My favorite musician today is _____ .

9. Is Batman a _____ ?

10. The best book I ever read was _____ .

11. Tonight's practice session became _____ but _____ .

12. Our neighbor brought home _____ .

13. With paper clips, you can make _____ .

14. Next Monday I begin my new _____ .

15. How soon will you finish _____ ?

THE SUBJECT COMPLEMENT

21   A *subject complement* is a noun, pronoun, or adjective that follows a linking verb. It describes or explains the simple subject.

There are two kinds of subject complements—the *predicate nominative* and the *predicate adjective.*

(1)   **A *predicate nominative* is a noun or pronoun in the predicate that explains or identifies the subject of the sentence.**

EXAMPLES   Termites are dangerous **pests.**

               The new attorney general is **she.**

               Mario is a very talented **musician.**

(2)   **A *predicate adjective* is an adjective in the predicate that modifies the subject of the sentence.**

EXAMPLES   The wind feels **cold.** [cold wind]

               The ground is **wet.** [wet ground]

Subject complements may be compound.

EXAMPLES   Two great songwriters were **Richard Rodgers** and **Oscar Hammerstein II.** [compound predicate nominatives]

               The pizza is **hot** and **spicy.** [compound predicate adjectives]

To find the subject complement in an interrogative sentence, rearrange the sentence to make a statement.

EXAMPLE   Was Barbra Streisand the director?

             Barbra Streisand was the **director.** [predicate nominative]

To find the subject complement in an imperative sentence, insert the understood subject *you.*

EXAMPLE   Be proud of your achievements!

             (You) Be **proud** of your achievements! [predicate adjective]

EXERCISE 13   Identifying Subject Complements

In each of the following sentences, underline the subject complement. On the line before the sentence, write *p.n.* for *predicate nominative* or *p.a.* for *predicate adjective.* [Hint: Some sentences may contain compound subject complements.]

EX. <u>p.a.</u>   1. The woods were <u>full</u> of wildflowers and animals.

_____   1. Marah is a canoeing counselor at a camp in Maine.

_____   2. Most of the campers are boys and girls from big cities.

_____   3. At first, some of the new arrivals seem a little scared and shy of the woods of Maine.

_____   4. To most of them, canoes seem dangerous.

_____   5. Marah is patient with these new wilderness campers.

_____   6. She becomes their guide to new experiences.

_____   7. Many rivers and river valleys in northern Maine are home to bears, moose, and other wild creatures.

_____   8. With Marah's help, children from the city become skilled and knowledgeable about the treasures of the wilderness.

_____   9. I was one of Marah's first campers, twelve years ago.

_____   10. Thanks to Marah, I am now a seasoned wilderness traveler and the author of two books about the rivers of Maine.

EXERCISE 14   Writing Subject Complements

Complete each sentence below by adding a subject complement. Add any other words that you feel are necessary to make your sentences clear. On the line before each word group, identify the complement in your completed sentence. Write *p.n.* for *predicate nominative* or *p.a.* for *predicate adjective*. [Hint: Some sentences need a compound complement.]

EX. <u>p.a.</u> 1. The river was <u>wide</u> and <u>deep</u>.

_____ 1. Suddenly, the sky became _____ .

_____ 2. My favorite food is _____ .

_____ 3. Is that man _____; or _____?

_____ 4. Nancy looked _____; but _____ .

_____ 5. The winner of the race was _____ .

_____ 6. Two inventions that changed the world are _____; and _____ .

_____ 7. Remain _____ to your friends.

_____ 8. The mountains appear _____ yet _____ .

_____ 9. Today the weather seems _____ .

_____ 10. Is Ms. Ramillo a _____?

OBJECTS

Objects are complements that do not refer to the subject.

2m   A *direct object* is a noun or pronoun that receives the action of the verb or shows the result of the action. It answers the question "Whom?" or "What?" after an action verb.

EXAMPLES   Gina called **me.** [Gina called *whom*? *Me* is the direct object.]
Hot soup may burn your **throat.** [Hot soup may burn *what*? *Throat* is the direct object.]

Direct objects are never found in prepositional phrases.

EXAMPLES   Yosef rode the **horse.** [*Horse* is the direct object.]
Yosef rode on the **horse.** [*Horse* is part of the prepositional phrase *on the horse.*]

2n   An indirect object is a noun or pronoun that precedes the direct object and usually tells to *whom* or for *whom* (or to *what* or for *what*) the action of the verb is done.

EXAMPLES   The coach gave **Josh** and **him** awards. [*Josh* and *him* are the compound indirect object of the verb *gave*, telling *to whom the coach gave the awards.* The noun *awards* is the direct object.]
Juan built his **sister** a shelf for her books. [The noun *sister* is the indirect object of the verb *built*, telling *for whom Juan built a shelf.* The noun *shelf* is the direct object.]

If the word *to* or *for* is used, the noun or pronoun following it is part of a prepositional phrase and cannot be an indirect object.

PREPOSITIONAL PHRASE   I made a card **for you.**
INDIRECT OBJECT   I made **you** a card.
PREPOSITIONAL PHRASE   He gave the extra ticket **to Tom.**
INDIRECT OBJECT   He gave **Tom** the extra ticket.

EXERCISE 15   Identifying Direct Objects

Underline the direct object in each of the following sentences.

EX.   1.   George's father and mother, Mr. and Mrs. Ristevski, own the <u>Liberty Deli</u>.

1. Students from the university and staff from the hospital often buy lunch there.

2. Early each morning, Mrs. Ristevski bakes the bread for the deli sandwiches.

3. Twice a month, Mr. Ristevski makes his own sausage.

4. During the cold winter months, the neighbors especially like the convenient location of the delicatessen.

5. For twenty-five years the Ristevski family has owned and managed the delicatessen.

EXERCISE 16   Identifying Direct Objects and Indirect Objects

In each sentence below, underline the direct object once and the indirect object twice. Some sentences may not contain an indirect object. [Hint: Both direct objects and indirect objects may be compound.]

EX. 1. Ms. Sanchez gave <u>Trudy</u> and <u>us</u> <u>directions</u> to her office.

1. Can you loan Marley and Pat enough money for their tickets?

2. He left your jacket in the hall closet.

3. Dr. Fuller gave the children some good advice about poison ivy.

4. Please read me the opening paragraph of your composition.

5. Before the hike, Pierre gave each girl and boy trail maps.

6. At the wildlife park, we took photographs of zebras and monkeys.

7. Could you please show me the fastest route to Monterey?

8. Take Marshall Boulevard to the top of the hill and turn right.

9. I'll give you this book about interesting sights in Monterey.

10. Thank you very much, sir.

11. Amy Tan published her first novel in 1989.

12. Did you study the life of Sauk chief Black Hawk?

13. He teaches his students the concepts of t'ai chi ch'uan, a system of self-defense and meditation.

14. My grandfather visited three cities in the Southwest.

15. The archaeologist Howard Carter found Tutankhamen's tomb.

CLASSIFYING SENTENCES BY PURPOSE

2o Sentences may be classified as *declarative, imperative, interrogative,* or *exclamatory.*

(1) A *declarative* **sentence makes a statement. All declarative sentences are followed by periods.**

EXAMPLE   The famous painter Arshile Gorky was born in Armenia in 1904.

(2) An imperative sentence gives a command or makes a request. Imperative sentences are usually followed by periods. Very strong commands, however, may be followed by exclamation points.

EXAMPLES   Please shut the window.
Don't swim alone.
Watch out for the sharks!

Notice that a command or request has the understood subject *you.*

(3) An *interrogative* **sentence asks a question. Interrogative sentences are followed by question marks.**

EXAMPLE   What is your favorite poem?

(4) An *exclamatory* **sentence expresses strong feeling. Exclamatory sentences are always followed by exclamation points.**

EXAMPLES   That car is rolling down the hill!
What an incredible race that was!
I can't believe I won a trip to Paris!

EXERCISE 17   Identifying the Four Kinds of Sentences

Add the correct punctuation mark to the end of each of the following sentences. On the line before the sentence, indicate which type of sentence it is. Write *dec.* for *declarative, inter.* for *interrogative, imp.* for *imperative,* or *excl.* for *exclamatory.* [Hint: Some imperative sentences may end in exclamation points.]

EX.   *imp.*   1. Stop fighting at once!

_____ 1.   Have you seen all of the Indiana Jones movies

_____ 2.   The first one, *Raiders of the Lost Ark*, came out in 1981

_____ 3.   What a fantastic movie it was

_____ 4. Although audiences had seen Harrison Ford as Han Solo in *Star Wars*, he became a star when he took on the role of Indiana Jones

_____ 5. Call the video store, and ask if they have *Raiders of the Lost Ark* in stock

_____ 6. Wow, there must have been at least a billion snakes in that scene

_____ 7. Are you afraid of snakes

_____ 8. Watch out for the falling rocks, Indy

_____ 9. Critics did not give the second Indiana Jones movie, *Indiana Jones and the Temple of Doom*, the great reviews that they gave the first one

_____ 10. Did you think that Karen Allen was a better heroine than Kate Capshaw

EXERCISE 18   Writing the Four Kinds of Sentences

You are sitting in a restaurant. Suddenly you notice that the diner at the next table is a large penguin. On your own paper, write a dialogue that might take place between you and the penguin. Add stage directions if you wish. Write ten sentences, and use at least two examples of each of the four kinds of sentences. Label each of your sentences to identify its classification.

EX. 1. *Me: (with a puzzled expression) We don't usually see penguins in this neighborhood. (dec.)*

MODULE REVIEW

A. Identifying the Parts of a Sentence

In the paragraph below, classify each underlined word according to its function in the sentence. Write *s.* for *subject, p.n.* for *predicate nominative, d.o.* for *direct object, v.* for *verb, p.a.* for *predicate adjective*, and *i.o.* for *indirect object*.

d.o.

EX. Romesh Gunesekera has published a [1] <u>book</u> of short stories.

Romesh Gunesekera is a [1] <u>native</u> of Sri Lanka. [2] <u>Sri Lanka</u> is an island nation located

in the Indian Ocean. Gunesekera now [3] <u>lives</u> in London, where he has published

[4] <u>*Monkfish Moon.*</u> His book is quite [5] <u>good</u> in its blending of appearance and reality. Its

nine short [6] <u>stories</u> give [7] <u>readers</u> several interesting [8] <u>views</u> of life in Sri Lanka.

[9] <u>Some</u> of the stories are [10] <u>frightening.</u> They [11] <u>tell</u> of events related to Sri Lanka's

long and cruel civil war. Only the [12] <u>setting</u>, however, will seem [13] <u>unfamiliar</u> to readers

outside of Sri Lanka. All of the stories contain complex [14] <u>characters</u> and vivid details.

Because Gunesekera [15] <u>has based</u> this excellent [16] <u>collection</u> of stories on his native

land, he has given the [17] <u>East</u> and the West a new and powerful [18] <u>link</u>. His book

[19] <u>is</u> both a masterpiece of literature and a [20] <u>tribute</u> to a beautiful and complex country.

B. Identifying and Punctuating the Four Kinds of Sentences

Add the correct punctuation mark to the end of each of the following sentences. On the line before the sentence, classify the sentence. Write *dec.* for *declarative, imp.* for *imperative, inter.* for *interrogative*, and *excl.* for *exclamatory*.

EX. _*imp.*_ 1. Please pass the salt

_____ 1. In 1991, Paul Sereno discovered a dinosaur fossil in Argentina

_____ 2. What a fierce animal that dinosaur must have been

_____ 3. Read the article about it in the September 1993 issue of *Earth* magazine

_____ 4. That dinosaur has been given the name *Eoraptor*

_____ 5. Did it live about 228 million years ago

_____ 6. Another dinosaur lived at about the same time

_____ 7. What was its name

_____ 8. It was called *Herrerasaurus*, and Sereno found its fossil in the same rock formation, along with *Eoraptor*

_____ 9. Do you believe that dinosaurs once roamed these woods

_____ 10. Wow, they must have been terrifying

C. Writing Sentences

On your own paper, write fifteen sentences according to the guidelines below. Underline the part or parts called for in the guidelines.

EX. 1. a declarative sentence with a compound verb

1. Alfonso Cuarón <u>wrote</u> and <u>directed</u> the movie *Roma.*

1. a declarative sentence with a predicate adjective

2. an interrogative sentence with a direct object

3. an interrogative sentence with a compound subject

4. an imperative sentence with an indirect object and a direct object

5. an imperative sentence that ends with a period

6. an imperative sentence that ends with an exclamation point

7. a declarative sentence with a compound indirect object and a direct object

8. an exclamatory sentence with a predicate adjective

9. a sentence that begins with *there* and contains a compound subject

10. a sentence with the understood subject *you*

11. a declarative sentence with a predicate nominative

12. an exclamatory sentence with a compound verb

13. a declarative sentence with a compound predicate nominative

14. an interrogative sentence with a compound verb

15. a sentence with the understood subject *you* and a compound verb

PREPOSITIONAL PHRASES

3a A *phrase* is a group of related words that is used as a single part of speech and does not contain both a predicate and its subject.

EXAMPLES   should have listened [verb phrase; no subject]

between Marika and Martin [prepositional phrase; no subject or verb]

3b A *prepositional phrase* is a group of words consisting of a preposition, a noun or pronoun that serves as the object of the preposition, and any modifiers of that object.

Some prepositions are made up of more than one word, like *in front of* or *prior to*. Also, an article or some other modifier often appears in a prepositional phrase.

EXAMPLES   Zahara built a model airplane **for her brother.** [The object of the preposition *for* is *brother*. The possessive pronoun *her* modifies *brother*.]

When will she give the birthday present **to him?** [The object of the preposition *to* is *him*.]

Our new bus stop is **in front of the supermarket.** [The object of the preposition *in front of* is *supermarket*. The adjective *the* modifies *supermarket*.]

Objects of prepositions may be compound.

EXAMPLES   Heavy snow fell **throughout the day and night**. [Both *day* and *night* are objects of the preposition *throughout*.]

In addition to you and me, six other people are coming. [The preposition *in addition to* has a compound object, *you* and *me*.]

Our new bus stop is **in front of the supermarket and the laundromat.** [The objects of the preposition *in front of* are *supermarket* and *laundromat*. The adjective *the* modifies *supermarket* and *laundromat*.]

EXERCISE 1   Identifying Prepositions and Their Objects

In each of the following sentences, underline the preposition, and draw an arrow from the preposition to its object.

EX. 1. Our voices echoed loudly <u>inside</u> the empty house.

1. Two of Mr. Johnson's children play the violin.

2. Today, you can buy almost anything from a catalog.

3. That girl with the catcher's mitt plays baseball well.

4. Imagine what the world would be like without television.

5. We spotted a doe and two fawns running across the grassy meadow.

6. The Forty-first and Forty-second Congresses had among their members the first African American representatives and the first African American senator.

7. The coach will award the medals at tonight's sports banquet.

8. Rain has been falling since dawn.

9. According to this article, nearly ten thousand Chinese immigrants helped construct the Central Pacific Railroad.

10. The baseball sailed over the fence, the street, and the parking garage.

EXERCISE 2   Writing Notes for TV

You are a writer for the show *Wildlife Facts*. Your next program is on snakes. Use the following notes to write ten sentences that might be used for the voice-over for this program. Include at least five prepositional phrases in your sentences. Underline the phrases and draw an arrow from the prepositions to their objects. Write these sentences on your own paper.

EX. 1.   True vipers are found in Africa and Eurasia.

NOTES

1. world's largest poisonous snake—king cobra

2. cobras—Malaysia, China, India, the Philippines

3. true vipers—Africa, Eurasia, and the East Indies

4. pit vipers—facial pits

5. rattlesnake—eats small animals, lifts tail to make sounds

6. African saw-scaled viper—rubs side scales together to produce rasping sound

7. North American sidewinder—moves sideways

8. water moccasin—southern swamps and bayous in North America

9. Indian cobra—hooded, lift up for battle

10. asp—also called Egyptian cobra

ADJECTIVE PHRASES AND ADVERB PHRASES

3c **A prepositional phrase that modifies a noun or pronoun is called an** *adjective phrase.*

Adjective phrases answer the same questions that adjectives answer: *What kind? Which one? How many?* or *How much?* An adjective phrase usually follows the noun or pronoun that it modifies. More than one phrase may modify the same word. An adjective phrase may also modify the object of another prepositional phrase.

EXAMPLES   The names **of the contest winners** will be announced tomorrow. [The phrase *of the contest winners* modifies the noun *names,* telling *which names.*]

Please bring me that big ball **of string in the garage.** [Both phrases modify the noun *ball. Of string* tells *what kind; in the garage* tells *which one.*]

The painting **of the girl with the dog** won first prize. [The phrase *of the girl* modifies the noun *painting,* telling *which painting.* The phrase *with the dog* modifies the object *girl,* telling *which girl.*]

EXERCISE 3   Identifying Adjective Phrases

Underline each adjective phrase in the sentences below. Draw an arrow to the word it modifies. [Note: Some sentences have more than one adjective phrase.]

EX. 1.   My grandparents tape-recorded stories of our family's history.

1. The walls around us were a brilliant yellow.

2. The flowers along the path are geraniums and petunias.

3. Leon took a picture of a blue heron next to a snowy egret.

4. The heavy winds of the storm spun the weather vane on the roof.

5. The cat ate all of the sardines in the tin.

6. *Hunger of Memory* is an autobiographical story by Richard Rodriguez.

7. The plays in the game were very exciting.

8. Mom opened the can of beans carefully.

9. Which of these books do you want?

10. The castle beside the ocean belonged to Prince Edward.

3d An *adverb phrase* is a prepositional phrase that modifies a verb, an adjective, or an adverb.

Adverb phrases answer the same questions that adverbs answer: *When? Where? How? To what extent?* (*How long? How many? How far?*)

EXAMPLES **Within a few minutes,** the concert will begin. [The phrase *Within a few minutes* modifies the verb phrase *will begin*, telling *when* the concert will begin.]
The water is deeper **on the far end**. [The phrase *on the far end* modifies the adjective *deeper*, telling *where* the water is deeper.]

Like adjective phrases, more than one adverb phrase may modify the same word.

EXAMPLE **With a final sprint,** Takara won the marathon **by three seconds.** [Both phrases modify the verb *won*. *With a final sprint* tells *how; by three seconds* tells *to what extent*.]

EXERCISE 4   Identifying Adverb Phrases and the Words They Modify

Underline the adverb phrases in the sentences below. Draw an arrow from each phrase to the word or words it modifies. [Note: Some sentences have more than one adverb phrase.]

EX. 1. After our classes, Germaine and I played basketball in the schoolyard.

1. Germaine pointed to the dark clouds that were gathering in the sky.

2. In a few minutes, thunder cracked loudly above our heads.

3. From the house, we watched the storm.

4. Lightning flashes appeared repeatedly for an hour.

5. Soon the lightning seemed closer to the house.

6. The whirligig was spinning out of control.

7. I thought the beets and carrots would be ripped out of the ground by the wind.

8. The rain grew from a drizzle to a downpour.

9. Germaine's dog Rosamunda hid under the bed.

10. His sister Elena ran through the house, pretending she was a rescue worker.

VERBALS AND VERB PHRASES

Verbals are formed from verbs. Like verbs, they may be modified by adverbs and may have complements. However, verbals are used as other parts of speech. There are three kinds of verbals: *participles, gerunds*, and *infinitives*.

3e   A *participle* is a verb form that can be used as an adjective.

EXAMPLE   The divers discovered **sunken** treasure off the coast of Key Largo.
[The participle *sunken*, formed from the verb *sink*, modifies the noun *treasure*.]

(1) *Present participles* end in *-ing*.

EXAMPLE   The photographer took a picture of the **laughing** baby.
[*Laughing* is a present participle modifying the noun *baby*.]

(2) *Past participles* usually end in *-d* or *-ed*. Other past participles are irregularly formed.

EXAMPLES   Please pass your **completed** test to the front of the room. [The past participle *completed* modifies the noun *test*.]
Her only son, **grown** and **gone** from home, visits her often. [The irregular past participles *grown* and *gone* modify the noun *son*.]

NOTE   Although participles are forms of verbs, they do not stand alone as verbs. However, a participle may be used with a helping verb to form a verb phrase. When a participle is used in this way, it is part of the verb and is therefore not an adjective.

EXAMPLES   Matthew **has been studying** Spanish.
Her son **is grown** and **has been gone** from home for years.

EXERCISE 5   Identifying Participles and the Words They Modify

Underline the participles used as adjectives in the following sentences. Then draw an arrow from each participle to the noun or pronoun that it modifies.

EX. 1. Splashing paint on the canvas, the artist created a masterpiece.

1.   The museum, known for its collection of modern art, has a new exhibit.

2.   Most of the pieces seen in this show are from private collections.

3. A crowd gathered around a sculpture of a group of people sitting on a bus.

4. The figures, assembled from plaster casts, seemed real.

5. Expressing his opinion loudly, one man obviously did not like the artist's work.

6. Framed and hung on the wall, an enormous picture of a mother and child captured the attention of many people.

7. For a long time, Marissa stood in front of the picture, staring and thinking.

8. Lecturing on the artists of the mid-1900s, the museum guide talked about the work of the sculptor Alexander Calder.

9. Some people believe that Calder's sculptures have a charming quality.

10. Connected with rods and wires and suspended in the air, Calder's mobiles are probably his most popular pieces.

EXERCISE 6   Choosing Appropriate Participles

On the line in each of the sentences below, write a participle that fits the meaning of the sentence.

EX. 1. The _____rising_____ tide washed over the beach.

1. The _____ sun cast a purple haze across the evening sky.

2. _____ her head, the baby fell asleep.

3. The whale, _____ suddenly out of the water, startled the people on the boat.

4. _____ in the sand, the clam was not visible to the hungry sea gulls.

5. We spent the day with our friends at the teen center, _____.

PARTICIPIAL PHRASES

3f A *participial phrase* is a phrase containing a participle and any complements or modifiers it may have.

A participial phrase should be placed as close as possible to the word it modifies. Otherwise the sentence may not make sense.

EXAMPLES **Hiking in the Sierra Nevada,** Paulo encountered a mountain lion. [The participle is modified by the prepositional phrase *in the Sierra Nevada*.]
Did you see that lioness **carrying her cubs?** [The participle has an object, *cubs*. The possesive pronoun *her* modifies *cubs*.]
The hiker, **acting quickly,** snapped a picture of the lion. [The participle is modified by the adverb *quickly*.]

EXERCISE 7   Identifying Participial Phrases

Underline the participial phrase in each of the following sentences. Draw an arrow from the participial phrase to the word or words the phrase modifies.

EX. 1.   Listening to the story of the princess and the frog, the children are enchanted.

1. Every Saturday morning, Shanti spends time at the library, telling stories to children.

2. Leaving their children at story hour, the parents run their errands.

3. Shanti reads with the children gathered in a circle around her.

4. The stories, chosen from among Shanti's own childhood favorites, are usually fairy tales and folk tales.

5. Enhanced by Shanti's unique style, each story delights the children.

6. Once, as I passed by the story-hour room, I overheard Shanti speaking gruffly.

7. Speaking in the voices of different characters, she was telling the story of the three little pigs.

8. The children held their breath when the wolf, huffing and puffing with all its might, tried to blow down the house of the third little pig.

9. The house built of bricks did not fall down, of course, and the pig survived.

10. Clapping and cheering at the end, the children showed how much they loved that folk tale.

EXERCISE 8   Identifying Participles and Participial Phrases

Underline each participle or participial phrase in the paragraph below. Draw an arrow from the participial phrase to the word or words that it modifies.

EX. [1] Underline: *Using an old tale*, a poet provides a different view of a familiar character.

[1] Thinking about tomorrow's assignment, I decided to talk about a poem.

[2] Skimming through my literature book, I came across an interesting poem titled "The Builders." [3] The poem, written by Sara Henderson Hay, does not actually identify its topic—"The Three Little Pigs." [4] The speaker of the poem is the pig who built his house of bricks, protecting himself from the starving wolf. [5] The pig, recalling recent events, tells the story in a scolding tone. [6] He points out that he told his brothers to build with bricks, but, being stubborn, they wouldn't listen to him. [7] The pig seems to be sorry that his brothers are gone, having been eaten by the wolf. [8] Having heard "The Three Little Pigs" so many times as a child, I found much to say about Hay's poem.

[9] Looking for something to use as my first prop, I found a shoebox in my closet.

[10] The shoebox, painted with a pattern of small bricks, would represent the pig's house.

3g   **A *gerund* is a verb form ending in *–ing* that is used as a noun.**

SUBJECT	**Walking** is good exercise.
PREDICATE NOMINATIVE	My favorite activity at the beach is **snorkeling**.
DIRECT OBJECT	Mom enjoys **golfing**.
OBJECT OF A PREPOSITION	A sturdy, thick-soled shoe is recommended for **hiking**.

Like nouns, gerunds may be modified by adjectives and adjective phrases.

DIRECT OBJECT	I watched **the incredible** diving **of the Olympic gold-medal winner.** [The article *the*, the adjective *incredible*, and the adjective phrase *of the Olympic gold-medal winner* modify the gerund *diving*.]
SUBJECT	**The sloppy** writing **of the note** made it impossible to understand. [The article *The*, the adjective *sloppy*, and the adjective phrase *of the note* modify the gerund *writing*.]

Like verbs, gerunds may also be modified by adverbs and adverb phrases.

SUBJECT	Cheering **loudly at the game** gave Geraldo a sore throat. [The gerund *Cheering* is modified by both the adverb *loudly* (telling *how*) and the adverb phrase *at the game* (telling *where*).]
DIRECT OBJECT	I would enjoy sitting **quietly for a while**. [The gerund *sitting* is modified by both the adverb *quietly* (telling *how*) and the adverb phrase *for a while* (telling *for how long*).]

Gerunds, like present participles, end in *–ing*. To be a gerund, a verbal must be used as a noun. In the following sentence, three words end in *–ing*, but only one of them is a gerund.

EXAMPLE	**Thinking** about the trip, Earline was **packing** suitable clothes for **sightseeing**. [*Thinking* is a present participle modifying *Earline*. *Packing* is part of the verb phrase *was packing*. Only *sightseeing*, used as the object of the preposition *for*, is a gerund.]

EXERCISE 9   Identifying and Classifying Gerunds

Underline the gerunds in the following sentences. On the line before each sentence, identify how each is used. Write *s.* for *subject, p.n.* for *predicate nominative, d.o.* for *direct object*, or *o.p.* for *object of a preposition*.

EX. __*s*__ 1. Fishing relaxes my dad.

_____ 1. Tomás enjoys gardening.

_____ 2. Bicycling is a sport that can be enjoyed at any age.

_____ 3. After the accident, she was bothered by a painful throbbing in her knee.

_____ 4. My favorite part of graduation was the singing, but Dad liked the speeches better.

_____ 5. Running in a marathon is Aretha's goal.

_____ 6. Acting in such plays as *Othello* and *The Emperor Jones* earned national attention for the renowned African American actor Paul Robeson.

_____ 7. On a hot day like today, the only work I want to do is writing.

_____ 8. The new puppies enjoy chasing each other playfully around the house.

_____ 9. When we went to Mexico, we took along a Spanish-English dictionary for translating.

_____ 10. Nestled in our sleeping bags, we heard the howling of a coyote, which sounded lonely to me.

EXERCISE 10   Writing About Hobbies

On the lines below, write five sentences about hobbies or activities that you enjoy. In each sentence, use a gerund, and underline it. In the space above the gerund, label its use in the sentence. Write *s.* for *subject, p.n.* for *predicate nominative, d.o.* for *direct object*, or *o.p.* for *object of a preposition*.

             s.

EX. 1. <u>*Playing*</u> *the Japanese game Go is fun.*

1. _____

    _____

2. _____

    _____

3. _____

    _____

4. _____

    _____

5. _____

    _____

GERUND PHRASES

3h   A *gerund phrase* contains a gerund and any modifiers or complements it may have.

SUBJECT	**The loud roaring of the wind** could be heard inside the cabin. [The gerund *roaring* is modified by the article *The*, the adjective *loud*, and the prepositional phrase *of the wind*.]
DIRECT OBJECT	Thelma enjoyed **racing swiftly on her bike**. [The gerund *racing* is modified by the adverb *swiftly* and by the prepositional phrase *on her bike*.]
PREDICATE NOMINATIVE	His hobby is **sending friends old postcards**. [The gerund *sending* has a direct object, *postcards*, and an indirect object, *friends*.]
OBJECT OF A PREPOSITION	She improved her composition by **rewriting the last paragraph**. [The gerund *rewriting* has a direct object, *paragraph*.]

NOTE   Whenever a noun or a pronoun comes before a gerund, the possessive form should be used.

EXAMPLES   The **parrot's** endless squawking made us laugh.
The **Her** cooking has really improved.

EXERCISE 11   Identifying and Classifying Gerund Phrases

Underline the gerund phrases in the following sentences. On the line before each sentence, identify how each phrase is used. Write *s.* for *subject, p.n.* for *predicate nominative, d.o.* for *direct object*, or *o.p.* for *object of a preposition*.

EX.   *s.* 1. <u>Traveling to exotic places</u> would be fun.

_____   1.   The people on the Samoan island of Upolu in the South Pacific showed their hospitality to the magazine photographer by welcoming her warmly.

_____   2.   The photographer's job was taking pictures of the island's scenery for a travel article.

_____   3.   She liked talking to the people about their remote South Pacific island.

_____   4.   Swimming in the warm waters of Upolu is possible all year.

_____   5.   A popular entertainment on the island is torch dancing.

_____ 6. Tourists enjoy diving from the reef.

_____ 7. Almost one hundred years ago, writer Robert Louis Stevenson found paradise by sailing to the island of Upolu.

_____ 8. Finding an island paradise is the dream of many writers.

_____ 9. After chartering a yacht, Robert Louis Stevenson set sail in search of his dream island.

_____ 10. Flying to Apia, the capital of Samoa, is the fastest and simplest way to reach this dream island today.

_____ 11. Driving over Cross Island Road takes you from one coast to the other.

_____ 12. Moving from Los Angeles to Polynesia must be a big change.

_____ 13. Losing your job might cause you to make such a move.

_____ 14. A way to honor the local leaders is by taking a Samoan name.

_____ 15. I don't know if I'd like moving to Samoa, but I'd vacation there if I could afford it.

EXERCISE 12 Working Cooperatively to Write Sentences with Gerund Phrases

Working with a partner, create ten sentences that use the gerund phrases below. Write on your own paper. Underline each gerund phrase, and write above the phrase _s._ for _subject_, _p.n._ for _predicate nominative_, _d.o._ for _direct object_, or _o.p._ for _object of a preposition_.

EX. 1. throwing the javelin

         _s._

   1. _Throwing the javelin_ was the second field event on the schedule.

1. putting on my running shoes

2. pole-vaulting at the track meet

3. pushing off from the starting block

4. firing the starting gun

5. passing the baton

6. running a marathon

7. crossing the finish line

8. lying on the grass to rest

9. landing in the sandpit

10. cheering for the athletes

INFINITIVES AND INFINITIVE PHRASES

3i   **An *infinitive* is a verb form, usually preceded by *to*, that can be used as a noun, an adjective, or an adverb.**

NOUNS   **To sing** with a rock band is Jon's dream. [*To sing* is the subject of the sentence.]

I had hoped **to finish** my story, but Joey's plan was **to leave** early. [*To finish* is the direct object of the verb phrase *had hoped*. *To leave* is the predicate nominative.]

ADJECTIVE   The person **to ask** is the information director. [*To ask* modifies the noun *person*.]

ADVERB   Eager **to rest**, we sat down on the grass. [*To rest* modifies the adjective *eager*.]

3j   **An *infinitive phrase* consists of an infinitive together with its modifiers and complements.**

NOUN   **To find a job quickly** is Rita's goal. [The phrase is the subject of the sentence. The infinitive has a direct object, *job*, and is modified by the adverb *quickly*.]

ADJECTIVE   Roses are the flowers **to give for a special occasion**. [The phrase modifies the predicate nominative *flowers*. The infinitive is modified by the adverb phrase *for a special occasion*.]

ADVERB   He seemed afraid **to say a word**. [The phrase modifies the predicate adjective *afraid* and has a direct object, *word*.]

An infinitive may have a subject. The infinitive, together with its subject, complements, and modifiers, is sometimes called an *infinitive clause*.

EXAMPLE   Mom asked **me to buy milk on my way home**. [*Me* is the subject of the infinitive *to buy*.]

Sometimes the *to* of the infinitive is omitted in a sentence.

EXAMPLE   Will you help me **find** my missing watch?

EXERCISE 13   Identifying and Classifying Infinitives

Underline the infinitives in the sentences below. On the line before each sentence, identify how each infinitive is used. Write *n.* for *noun, adj.* for *adjective,* or *adv.* for *adverb.*

EX. __*n.*__   1.   <u>To be</u> a member of the hockey team was important to Chris.

_____   1.   Slow to start, the car was old and unreliable.

_____   2.   Does anyone wish to respond to the mayor's comments?

_____   3.   Dan is the person to follow, because he always knows exactly where he's going.

_____   4.   Mr. Petrakis ran to catch his train so that it would not leave without him.

_____   5.   We left our seats to get some popcorn.

EXERCISE 14   Identifying and Classifying Infinitive Phrases

Underline the infinitive phrases in the sentences below. On the line before each sentence, identify how the infinitive phrase is used. Write *n.* for *noun, adj.* for *adjective,* or *adv.* for *adverb.*

EX. __*n.*__ 1.   <u>To make pizza</u> requires some planning ahead.

_____   1.   Earlier, Luisa and Josh went to get the ingredients at the market.

_____   2.   To prepare the most delicious pizza ever was their objective.

_____   3.   They had already decided to heap lots of fresh vegetables on the pizza.

_____   4.   They needed advice from Luisa's mother on the best way to make the tomato sauce.

_____   5.   She was happy to share her old family recipe with them.

_____   6.   To stretch the dough properly was another technique that she demonstrated for them.

_____   7.   Once the dough was stretched and the sauce was cooked, Luisa and Josh were ready to assemble their pizza.

_____   8.   Josh asked Luisa to ladle the sauce on the dough.

_____   9.   After mushrooms, peppers, artichokes, onions, and cheese were piled on the dough, it was time to bake the pizza in a very hot oven.

_____   10.   Then they invited some friends for dinner, because, Josh said, "Pizza is a food to eat with friends!"

MODULE 3: THE PHRASE
REVIEW EXERCISE

A. Identifying and Classifying Prepositional Phrases

Underline all the prepositional phrases in the paragraph below. In the space above each phrase, identify how the phrase is used. Write *adj.* for *adjective* and *adv.* for *adverb*.

EX. [1] I. M. Pei is just one *of the many architects* whose work enhances city landscapes worldwide.

[1] I. M. Pei, born in Canton, China, in 1917, is the son of a successful Chinese banker. [2] Pei came to the United States to study architectural engineering when he was eighteen years old. [3] Because of a war between China and Japan, Pei could not go home after his college graduation. [4] He obtained a master of architecture degree from Harvard University and, in 1948, joined the staff of an important architectural firm. [5] Before this time, Pei had never designed any actual buildings, but the head of the firm was impressed by Pei's architectural drawings. [6] He wanted Pei on his staff. [7] With this important job, Pei had his chance to alter modern urban environments. [8] Many cities are more beautiful because of Pei's decision to join that firm. [9] Among the buildings he has designed are the Mile High Center in Denver, Colorado, the East Building of the National Gallery of Art, and the Dallas City Hall. [10] If you are looking at Boston's Government Center or Montreal's Place Ville Marie, you are looking at Pei's designs.

B. Identifying and Classifying Verbals and Verbal Phrases

Underline the verbal or verbal phrase in each of the following sentences. On the line before each sentence, identify the verbal or verbal phrase. Write *ger.* for *gerund, ger. phr.* for *gerund phrase, inf.* for *infinitive, inf. phr.* for *infinitive phrase, part.* for *participle,* or *part. phr.* for *participial phrase.*

EX. _*ger. phr.*_ 1. <u>Imagining a world without computers</u> is impossible for me.

_____ 1. The photo in the book showed bats hanging upside down.

_____ 2. Although I've tried, I can't seem to take a really good photograph of a sunset.

_____ 3. Theo's one passion is acting.

_____ 4. Lost, the young boy worried that he might never find his way home.

_____ 5. She had a question she wanted to ask.

_____ 6. We came to a tidal pool where we saw crabs, shrimp, and other ocean creatures swimming around.

_____ 7. The fire was about to spread to other buildings when the fire trucks arrived.

_____ 8. Walking beneath the bridge, we could hear the rumble of the train on the tracks above.

_____ 9. It seems obvious, but the only way you'll ever become a better dancer is by dancing more.

_____ 10. The growling lion frightened away the birds.

C. Writing an Email with Verbals and Verbal Phrases

You are on a space team that is exploring Saturn. Once a month, you are allowed to send home an interplanetary email ten sentences long. Write an email to your friend. Explain what you've been doing. Describe your most exciting discoveries. You may also want to tell your friend what you do for relaxation and entertainment on your days off. Include at least one of each type of verbal and verbal phrase. Underline each verbal or verbal phrase in your sentences. Identify each verbal or verbal phrase by writing *ger.* for *gerund, ger. phr.* for *gerund phrase, inf.* for *infinitive, inf. phr.* for *infinitive phrase, part.* for *participle*, or *part. phr.* for *participial phrase*.

> *part. phr.*
>
> EX. *Being involved in interplanetary exploration,* I have a new appreciation of our entire universe.

MODULE 3: THE PHRASE

APPOSITIVES AND APPOSITIVE PHRASES

3k An *appositive* is a noun or a pronoun given beside another noun or pronoun to identify or explain it.

EXAMPLES   My friend **Janet** invited me to her family's cabin. [The noun *Janet* identifies the noun *friend*.]

Linda Ronstadt, a popular **singer,** has recorded an album of Mexican songs. [The noun *singer* explains the noun *Linda Ronstadt*.]

3l An *appositive phrase* is made up of the appositive and its modifiers.

EXAMPLES   Joseph, **star pitcher of our baseball team,** sprained his wrist.

The movie *La Bamba* was based on the life of Ritchie Valens, **one of the great rock musicians of the 1950s.**

NOTE   An appositive phrase usually follows the noun or pronoun it refers to. Sometimes, however, the appositive precedes the noun or pronoun explained.

EXAMPLE   **A volunteer worker at the library,** Pamela knows exactly where to look for a book.

Appositives and appositive phrases are usually set off by commas unless the appositive is a single word closely related to the preceding noun or pronoun. Commas are always used with appositives that refer to proper nouns.

ESSENTIAL   Our cat **Snowball** likes to sleep under the couch. [The writer has more than one cat. The appositive is necessary to tell which cat is referred to.]

NONESSENTIAL   Our cat, **Snowball,** likes to sleep under the couch. [The writer has only one cat. The appositive is not necessary to identify the cat.]

EXERCISE 15   Identifying Appositives and Appositive Phrases

In the following sentences, underline all appositive phrases once. Underline twice the word or words an appositive phrase identifies or explains.

EX. 1. Summer, my favorite time of year, is a great time for hiking.

1.   The magazine *Music* is a guide to the enjoyment of classical music.

2.   One dessert on the menu, the fresh fruit, is not available today.

3. This article discusses the life and works of Langston Hughes, a poet, novelist, and short-story writer.

4. Tanya wants to become an occupational therapist, a person who treats people with sports injuries and other kinds of injuries.

5. Marjorie, the director of the senior community center, is looking for volunteers to work at the center two days a week.

6. A nuisance to everyone, the mosquitoes seem to be bigger and hungrier this summer.

7. Have you ever played charades, a game in which you have to act out titles for your teammates to guess?

8. My sister Kimiko just got her driver's license.

9. Ina returned the blouse to the store for a refund, twenty-two dollars.

10. What did you think of the movie *Harry Potter and the Goblet of Fire?*

EXERCISE 16   Adding Appositives

On the line in each of the sentences below, write an appositive or appositive phrase that fits the meaning of the sentence.

EX. 1. Fluffy, _____*my house cat*_____, lapped some milk and curled up again on my lap.

1. My friend _____ and I are going to the library.

2. Our library, _____, is open on Saturdays.

3. We are giving a presentation, _____, in class.

4. My parents, _____, say television is harmful.

5. We would like to see some research, _____, to decide for ourselves.

6. The jury, _____, reached a verdict.

7. My sister _____ sang in the choir.

8. Is your favorite dish, _____, being served?

9. James asked everyone where his dog _____ had gone.

10. Two students, _____ and _____, won the contest.

MODULE 3: THE PHRASE
MODULE REVIEW

A. Identifying and Classifying Prepositional Phrases

Underline each prepositional phrase in the paragraph below. Then draw an arrow from the phrase to the word or words it modifies. In the space above the phrase, write *adj.* for *adjective phrase* or *adv.* for *adverb phrase*. A sentence may have more than one phrase.

EX. [1] The concerts always start with "The Star-Spangled Banner."

[1] Every Friday evening during the summer, something very special happens in our seaside town. [2] That's when Mr. Turner, who is eighty-four years old, takes his place in front of the Pleasantville Town Band. [3] For forty-six years Mr. Turner has been leading the band in rousing songs that celebrate and reflect the American spirit. [4] Each Friday night, thousands gather at the Vernon Turner Bandstand and watch Mr. Turner conduct. [5] Mr. Turner has loved music throughout his life. [6] As a college student he studied music, and he eventually became a music teacher in the Pleasantville area. [7] Although Mr. Turner has considered retirement several times, the adoration he receives from band and community members keeps him working.

B. Identifying Verbals and Appositives

On the line before each of the following sentences, identify the italicized word or word group. Write *prep.* for *preposition, part.* for *participle, ger.* for *gerund, inf.* for *infinitive,* or *app.* for *appositive.*

EX. *inf.* 1. Molly wants *to keep* a journal during the summer.

_____ 1. The *stolen* notebook was never recovered, and so the results of his experiments remain a mystery.

_____ 2. Were you planning *to attend* the junior class play?

_____ 3. Hector described his trip, the *one* that he took to Mexico.

_____ 4. *Instead of* taking the bus, let's walk to school today.

_____ 5. Many people associate *knitting* with grandmothers, but my uncle Tim knits sweaters that are works of art.

C. Writing Sentences with Phrases

On your own paper, write ten sentences, following the directions given below. Underline your phrase in each sentence. If your phrase is a modifier, draw two lines under the word or words it modifies.

EX. 1. Use an adjective phrase to modify the subject of a sentence.

    1. *The <u>tree</u> <u>in front of our house</u> is a weeping cherry tree.*

1. Use an adjective phrase to modify the object of a preposition.

2. Use an adverb phrase to modify an adjective.

3. Use an adverb phrase to modify a verb.

4. Use a participial phrase to modify a subject.

5. Use a participial phrase to modify a direct object.

6. Use a gerund phrase as the object of a preposition.

7. Use a gerund phrase as a predicate nominative.

8. Use an infinitive phrase as a noun.

9. Use an infinitive phrase as an adjective.

10. Use an appositive phrase beside a direct object.

D. Working Cooperatively to Create a Cluster

Work with a partner to think of situations that are associated with smiles and frowns. On your own paper, fill in a prewriting cluster for smiles and frowns. Use gerund and prepositional phrases, and include at least one infinitive or infinitive phrase in your cluster.

EX.

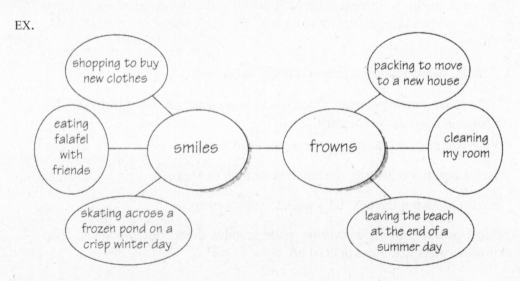

KINDS OF CLAUSES

4a A *clause* is a group of words that contains a verb and its subject and is used as part of a sentence.

4b An *independent* (or *main*) *clause* expresses a complete thought and can stand by itself as a sentence.

EXAMPLES   Elena is studying astronomy.
              She wants to be an astronaut.

Each independent clause has its own subject and verb and expresses a complete thought. These clauses can be joined by a comma and a coordinating conjunction such as *and, but, or, for, so*, or *yet*. They could also be written with a semicolon between them or with a semicolon followed by a conjunctive adverb and a comma.

EXAMPLES   Elena is studying astronomy, and she wants to be an astronaut.
              Elena is studying astronomy; she wants to be an astronaut.
              Elena is studying astronomy; indeed, she wants to be an astronaut.

4c A *subordinate* (or *dependent*) *clause* does not express a complete thought and cannot stand alone.

A subordinate clause must be joined to at least one independent clause to express a complete thought. Words such as *whom, because, what, if*, and *when* signal the beginning of a subordinate clause.

SUBORDINATE CLAUSES   if the fog lifts

                         when the show begins

                         whom we have met before

SENTENCES   **If the fog lifts,** we can go sailing.

               Did you ask **when the show begins?**

               Sumio, **whom we have met before,** will take us to the site.

EXERCISE 1   Identifying Independent and Subordinate Clauses

In the following paragraph, identify each italicized clause. On the line before each sentence, write *indep.* for *independent* or *sub.* for *subordinate*.

  EX. [1] __*indep.*__ Before 2000 B.C. *there were no post offices for the general public.*

[1] _____ Egypt is most likely *where the first postal system was developed*. [2] _____ *Postal systems were developed* because ancient governments needed to relay messages. [3] _____ The central government could control provincial administration only *if there was a system of communication linking the capital and the provinces*. [4] _____ Later postal systems employed relay stations, *which would provide fresh horses and riders*. [5] _____ *Since this idea is so practical*, it was probably thought of quite soon.

[6] _____ Evidence *that postal relay stations were used*, however, is no older than 500 B.C. [7] _____ *The Roman Empire needed a postal system* because it was so enormous in every regard. [8] _____ The Roman Empire's postal system was important enough *that it was preserved by the succeeding Islamic Empire*.

[9] _____ In the Middle Ages, *additional postal routes were set up privately* so traders could conduct business. [10] _____ *It was not until the middle of the sixteenth century A.D.* that private persons and businesses were allowed to use the government's postal system. [11] _____ *United Parcel Service and Federal Express are contemporary versions of these privately run postal systems*.

[12] _____ Private citizens' using the postal system was begun in Europe by the prince Thurn und Taxis, *who ran the Imperial postal system of his country*.

[13] _____ *This practice began the era of the postage stamp*, which was invented as a way to charge private persons who sent mail. [14] _____ *Before the stamp was invented*, people had to pay to receive mail sent to them.

[15] _____ Some people today want to revert to this practice *because they think it would cut down on junk mail*.

THE ADJECTIVE CLAUSE

4d An *adjective clause* is a subordinate clause that modifies a noun or a pronoun.

An adjective clause follows the word it modifies. If a clause is essential to the meaning of the sentence, it is not set off with commas. If a clause only gives additional information and is nonessential to the meaning of a sentence, it is set off by commas.

EXAMPLES   The pond, **which is a landing place for migrating birds**, lies in a protected area. [The clause *which is a landing place for migrating birds* is not necessary to identify *pond* and is set off by commas.]

Baseball is the sport **that I like best**. [The clause *that I like best* is essential to the meaning of the sentence and, therefore, is not set off by commas.]

Adjective clauses are usually introduced by ***relative pronouns.*** These words relate an adjective clause to the word that the clause modifies.

Relative Pronouns				
that	which	who	whom	whose

EXAMPLES   Sarah, **who had lived in the Philippines,** still had many friends there. [The relative pronoun *who* relates the adjective clause to *Sarah. Who* is the subject of the adjective clause.]

Stephen Hawking is a scientist **whom I greatly admire**. [The relative pronoun *whom* relates the adjective clause to the subject. *Whom* is the direct object of the verb *admire* in the adjective clause.]

The author, **whose new book was published this week,** spoke to our class. [The relative pronoun *whose* relates the adjective clause to *author. Whose* is used as a possessive pronoun in the adjective clause.]

In many cases, the relative pronoun in the clause may be omitted.

EXAMPLE   Here is the video **you wanted**. [The relative pronoun *that* is understood. *That* relates the adjective clause to *video* and is the direct object in the adjective clause.]

EXERCISE 2   Identifying Adjective Clauses

Underline the ten adjective clauses in the paragraph below.

EX. [1] Cesar Chavez, <u>who was born in 1927</u>, helped migrant workers improve their lives.

[1] Cesar Chavez, who spent much of his life trying to improve the lives of migrant farm workers, believed in the power of nonviolent protests. [2] His parents owned a store, which they lost in the Great Depression of the 1930s. [3] The Chavez family moved to California and joined the migrant workers who moved throughout the state, harvesting crops. [4] Chavez learned firsthand about the miserable conditions which these people had to endure. [5] He searched for ideas and methods that would improve the lives of farm laborers. [6] He organized a boycott of California grapes that spread throughout the United States. [7] The boycott helped workers win a contract, which was the first in the history of farm laborers. [8] In 1968, Chavez began a fast that lasted twenty-five days. [9] It was the first of three times he fasted to protest the low pay and poor working conditions of the farm laborer. [10] Chavez, who died in 1993, saw several improvements in farm labor practices in his lifetime.

EXERCISE 3   Revising Sentences by Supplying Adjective Clauses

Revise the following pairs of sentences by substituting an adjective clause for one of the sentences. Write the revisions on your own paper.

EX. 1. We were lucky to see a minke whale. This whale rarely swims into this area.

   1. *We were lucky to see a minke whale, which rarely swims into this area.*

1. Lian planned the menu for the fund-raiser. The fund-raiser was successful.

2. Two reporters moderated the debate. The reporters are well known.

3. Amy and Cheng questioned the results of the experiment. This experiment was the first.

4. The hikers agreed to try a less difficult route. The hikers were tired.

5. The audience became restless during the presentation. The presentation was long.

THE ADVERB CLAUSE

4e An *adverb clause* is a subordinate clause that modifies a verb, an adjective, or an adverb.

An adverb clause tells *how, when, where, why, how much, to what extent* or *under what condition* the action of the main verb takes place. Adverb clauses are introduced by *subordinating conjunctions.*

Common Subordinating Conjunctions			
after	because	since	when
although	before	so that	whenever
as	even though	than	where
as if	if	though	wherever
as long as	in order that	unless	whether
as soon as	once	until	while

EXAMPLES   **After the judge announced her decision,** the attorneys held a press conference. [The adverb clause *after the judge announced her decision* tells *when* the attorneys held a press conference.]

We will go on to the summit **if the good weather holds**. [*If the good weather holds* tells *under what condition* we will go to the summit.]

Because traffic was so heavy, the Parks decided to take a different route. [*Because traffic was so heavy* tells *why* the Parks decided to take a different route.]

NOTE   Introductory adverb clauses are usually set off by commas.

EXAMPLE   If you want to come, call me.

EXERCISE 4   Identifying and Classifying Adverb Clauses

Underline the adverb clause in each of the following sentences. Above each adverb clause, write whether the clause tells *how, when, where, why, how much, to what extent*, or *under what condition.*

when
EX. 1. We go camping every year <u>before school starts</u>.

1. While we were camping in August, we saw a meteor shower.

2. Meteor showers occur when rock or iron particles called meteoroids enter earth's atmosphere from space.

3. As these particles enter the earth's atmosphere, they heat up and glow brightly.

4. We call the burning particles "shooting stars" even though they are not really stars.

5. Meteor showers are spectacular because you can see many shooting stars in one night.

6. November is a good month to watch for meteors because the Leonid meteor shower occurs every November.

7. Where space debris is abundant, the showers are more brilliant.

8. Unless you can get away from cities, light pollution makes it hard to see meteors.

9. Once we had driven far enough from the city, we started looking for a campsite.

10. After we viewed the sunset, we watched the sky and saw a fine show.

EXERCISE 5 Building Sentences That Have Adverb Clauses

On your own paper, write ten sentences, using a clause from the list below in each sentence. Do not use the same subordinate clause twice. In each sentence you create, underline the adverb clause once and the word or words it modifies twice. You may combine two of the clauses below or add words of your own.

EX. some people are always hungry   the lunch bags appear right away

   1. *Because some people are always hungry*, the lunch bags *appear* right away.

1. after we get to the Museum of Science	wherever no one can hear
2. where our class goes on an outing	because we left the parking lot
3. before we will allow radios with speakers	since some people are always hungry
4. as Mr. Henshaw gets off the bus	until we can agree on music
5. once Mr. Favaloro starts talking	as long as we meet at the cafeteria
6. while someone makes a joke	whenever we see a video of an animal
7. as if we agree	so that the bus can leave at nine o'clock
8. if Mr. Henshaw acts like a tour guide	as soon as we eat lunch
9. unless we ban radios with speakers	although Mr. Favaloro laughs hardest
10. in order that we eat lunch	when we scatter through the museum

THE NOUN CLAUSE

4f A *noun clause* is a subordinate clause used as a noun.

A noun clause may be used as a subject, a complement (predicate nominative, direct object, indirect object), or the object of a preposition.

SUBJECT	**What I liked best about my trip to Mexico** was seeing the Aztec ruins.
PREDICATE NOMINATIVE	The loser is **whoever has the final piece to the puzzle**.
DIRECT OBJECT	We thought we knew **what Kwam's gift would be**.
INDIRECT OBJECT	The chef will tell **whoever asks** the recipe for her specialty.
OBJECT OF A PREPOSITION	She carefully checked the applications of **whoever applied for the job**.

Noun clauses are usually introduced by *that, what, whatever, who, whoever, whom,* and *whomever*. Sometimes, however, noun clauses do not have an introductory word.

EXAMPLE   Joey wished he could join the group. [The introductory word *that* is understood.]

EXERCISE 6   Identifying and Classifying Noun Clauses

Underline each noun clause in the following paragraph. Above it, identify how it is used. Write *s.* for *subject, p.n.* for *predicate nominative, d.o.* for *direct object, i.o.* for *indirect object*, or *o.p.* for *object of a preposition*.

d. o.

EX. [1] My sister always said <u>that she did not like animals</u>.

[1] What changed her mind was her discovering a baby opossum in our backyard.

[2] She realized that it was too tiny to survive on its own. [3] She didn't know what to do

with it or who could help her. [4] That our town had a wildlife rescue center proved to be

the answer to her problem. [5] My sister carefully wrapped the baby opossum in

whatever soft rags were at hand and took it to the center. [6] The director told her the center would care for the opossum until it was old enough to return to the wild.

[7] My sister asked whoever was free many questions. [8] Now she is a volunteer at the

center, helping in whatever way she can. [9] A veterinarian is what she wants to be. [10]

Whatever animals she treats will be in good hands.

EXERCISE 7   Writing Sentences by Inserting Noun Clauses

On your own paper, add noun clauses to the sentences below. Then label the function of
the noun clause in each sentence.

EX. 1. Eliza told me *that Ramón is going to the carnival tonight. (d.o.)* (Use *that*)

1. _____

    _____ is a sad fact. (Use *that*.)

2. _____

    _____ had better tell me. (Use *whoever*.)

3. _____

    _____ is a good vacation. (Use *what*.)

4. Did you know _____

    _____ (Use *that*.)

5. Mom always gives _____

    _____ a reward. (Use *whoever*.)

6. The teacher limited test items to _____

    _____ .(Use *whatever*.)

7. _____

    _____ will probably always be a mystery to me. (Use *where*.)

8. The best answer is _____

    _____ . (Use *whatever*.)

9. Was your question _____

    _____ ? (Use *how*.)

10. We all wanted to know _____

    _____ . (Use *who*.)

4g According to their structure, sentences are classified as *simple, compound, complex,* and *compound-complex.*

(1) A *simple sentence* has one independent clause and no subordinate clauses. It may have a compound subject, a compound verb, and any number of phrases.

EXAMPLE After studying Russia and listening to their grandmother's stories, Tanya and Alexis decided to prepare a Russian meal for their friends.

(2) A *compound sentence* has two or more independent clauses but no subordinate clauses.

In effect, a compound sentence consists of two or more simple sentences joined by a comma and a coordinating conjunction, by a semicolon, or by a semicolon followed by a conjunctive adverb and a comma.

EXAMPLES They had eaten many of their grandmother's Russian specialties, **but** they had never prepared them.
Tanya's favorite was piroshki; Alexis liked dumplings, latkes, and blini.
They had watched their grandmother prepare these dishes; **consequently,** they knew it was a lot of work.

(3) A *complex sentence* has one independent clause and at least one subordinate clause.

EXAMPLES Tanya suggested that they also serve a soup, a salad, and Russian tea.
When they told their grandmother about their plans, she offered to help.

(4) A *compound-complex sentence* contains two or more independent clauses and at least one subordinate clause.

EXAMPLES Tanya and Alexis wanted to invite everyone who was interested in their plans, and so they had a long guest list.
Before the party began, the two had spent many hours cooking, and so had their grandmother, who said the feast was first-rate.

EXERCISE 8   Classifying Sentences According to Structure

Classify each sentence in the paragraph below. On the line before each sentence, write *simp.* for *simple, comp.* for *compound, cx.* for *complex,* and *cd.-cx.* for *compound-complex.*

EX. ___cx.___ [1] Machu Picchu, which is located on a mountaintop in Peru, was the capital city for the Incas a thousand years ago.

_____ [1] Built on a peak in the Andes and overlooking a deep canyon, the ancient city contains the ruins of four hundred houses, as well as temples, plazas, and palaces.

_____ [2] It was constructed of granite blocks; how the Incas, who had only simple tools, transported this stone up the steep mountain remains a puzzle. _____ [3] A Peruvian legend says that the ancient Incas were helped by angel architects who made the granite fall off cliffs and fly to the building site. _____ [4] Some modern engineers believe this explanation as much as any other! _____ [5] Incas lived in Machu Picchu until the population outgrew the food supply; then they moved the capital to Cuzco, which is on the western slope of the Andes. _____ [6] Machu Picchu was no longer inhabited, but perhaps it was not entirely forgotten. _____ [7] The Spaniards came to Peru hundreds of years after Machu Picchu was abandoned. _____ [8] The Spaniards, who were searching for gold, attempted to seize a convent where Inca women devoted their lives to the service of the Sun God. _____ [9] They found the convent empty; the women had vanished. _____ [10] Many Incas believed that the Sun God lifted the women into the sky; but after explorers discovered Machu Picchu in 1911, some people came to believe that the women took refuge there.

MODULE REVIEW

A. Classifying Subordinate Clauses

Classify each italicized clause in the paragraph below. Write *adj.* for *adjective, adv.* for *adverb*, or *n.* for *noun* above the clause.

                          adv.   adj.
EX. [1] *Although rock climbing looks difficult*, it is a sport [2] *that nearly everyone can try*.

The variety of the sport is [1] *what makes it open to anyone* [2] *who is interested*.

Rock climbing can be climbing [3] *in which the climber stays close to the ground without a rope or special gear*, or it can be big wall-climbing, a feat [4] *that requires much more training*. [5] *Although physical strength and coordination are useful*, expert climbers say [6] *that these are not all there is to climbing*. Determination and courage are also qualities [7] *that a climber must have*. [8] *What you need first of all* is an experienced teacher [9] *with whom you can climb*. [10] *After you have followed an expert up enough rocks*, you may be ready to lead a climb yourself.

B. Identifying and Classifying Clauses

In the following sentences, underline the subordinate clauses. On the line before each sentence, identify the way each clause is used. Write s. for *subject*, d.o. for *direct object*, i.o. for *indirect object*, p.n. for *predicate nominative*, o.p. for *object of a preposition*, adj. for *adjective*, or *adv.* for *adverb*. [Note: Some sentences have more than one clause.]

EX. ___*adv.*___ 1. <u>When Maryssa gave a report on frogs,</u> the class was fascinated.

_____ 1. I had always thought that frogs were boring.

_____ 2. What Maryssa described showed that she had done a lot of research.

_____ 3. She said that West Africa is home to the world's largest frog, which can grow to a length of three feet.

_____ 4. The smallest known frog is found in Cuba and is only one-half inch long when it is fully grown.

_____ 5. If a person could jump proportionately as far as one small North American frog, the world's long-jump record would be 215 feet.

_____ 6. Because eggs are easy prey, some frogs have developed interesting strategies for protecting their eggs.

_____ 7. It is the male parent of the Darwin's frog in South Africa who guards the eggs.

_____ 8. When the eggs show signs of life, the male frog swallows five to fifteen of them and holds them in his croaking sac until they hatch.

_____ 9. Maryssa also described a male frog who guards newly laid eggs by carrying them wound around his leg.

_____ 10. My favorite story was about the helmet frog, who uses its bony head as a door for its home inside a tree.

C. Rewriting a Paragraph to Include a Variety of Sentence Structures

After researching a topic for an essay, you have jotted down the draft of the paragraph below. On your own paper, rewrite the paragraph to improve its style. You will need to vary the sentence structure, and you may want to delete, reword, or add details. Write at least one sentence with each kind of structure: simple, compound, complex, and compound-complex. Be ready to identify the structure of each sentence you write.

1 Dr. Maria Montessori was a pioneer in the field of education.

2 She was also the first woman in Italy to attend medical school. She

3 was born in Italy in 1870. That year Italy became a nation. As a

4 teenager she was interested in mathematics. Her parents suggested

5 she become a teacher. This was practically the only career open to

6 women at that time. She decided that she wanted to attend medical

7 school. She was told this was impossible. She persisted and won

8 entrance to medical school. She even won scholarships. As the only

9   female student, she endured great hardships in medical school. She

10   graduated in 1896. After graduation, she worked at a psychiatric

11   clinic. She became interested in children with learning problems.

12   She came to believe that with the proper education, their lives

13   could improve. She became director of a school for children who

14   were considered hopeless. The progress of the children in her

15   school surprised everyone. She went on to develop theories of

16   education for all children. The equipment she designed for

17   teaching and her ideas about how young children learn are used

18   now in Montessori schools all over the world.

MODULE 5: AGREEMENT

SUBJECT-VERB AGREEMENT

Number is the form of a word that indicates whether the word is singular or plural.

5a **When a word refers to one person or thing, it is *singular* in number. When a word refers to more than one, it is *plural* in number.**

SINGULAR	plumber	mouse	I	chopstick
PLURAL	plumbers	mice	we	chopsticks

EXERCISE 1   Classifying Nouns and Pronouns by Number

In the sentences below, identify each italicized word by writing *sing.* for *singular* or *pl.* for *plural* above the word.

                       pl.   *sing.*

EX.   1.   The tiny *peaches* were carved from a *piece* of green jade.

1.   Cleon said that Irene and *he* can rehearse their *scenes* later.

2.   When the ball came flying toward the plate, *Vincente* swung the bat with all *his* strength.

3.   The political *cartoons* are usually on the editorial *page*.

4.   Simone Biles has certainly won a lot of *medals* and *awards* in gymnastic events!

5.   An auto *mechanic* can adjust your *brakes* easily.

6.   The new stained-glass *windows* replaced the *ones* that had been damaged during the hailstorm.

7.   Each person in the *class* created colorful *drawings* of people or animals.

8.   An antique silk *kimono* was displayed in a glass *case*.

9.   The driver asked *us* if *we* wanted to stop at Monticello.

10.   Corey is teaching his twin *sisters* how to ride *their* bikes.

5b **A verb should always agree with its subject in number.**

(1) Singular subjects take singular verbs.

EXAMPLE   **Julie kicks** the ball to me. [The singular verb *kicks* agrees with the singular subject *Julie*.]

(2) Plural subjects take plural verbs.

EXAMPLE   The **players run** toward the goal. [The plural verb *run* agrees with the plural subject *players*.]

Like single-word verbs, verb phrases also agree with their subjects. However, in a verb phrase, only the first helping (auxiliary) verb changes its form to agree with the subject.

EXAMPLES   **Maribeth has** been working on my campaign.
            Maribeth and **Eula have** been working on my campaign.

EXERCISE 2   Identifying Verbs That Agree in Number with Their Subjects

For each sentence below, underline the verb in parentheses that agrees with the subject.

EX.   1. First, the pilot (*checks*, *check*) the controls.

1. (*Has, Have*) you ever seen Alvin Ailey's ballet?

2. The Pachecos all (*laughs, laugh*) at the same jokes.

3. These folk tales (*is, are*) about how the world began.

4. First, the students (*picks, pick*) up their pencils.

5. Mama (*has, have*) made sopapillas for dessert.

6. Several trains (*runs, run*) on that track.

7. My youngest cousin (*spins, spin*) the dreidel first.

8. The Indian monetary system (*is, are*) based on the rupee, not the dollar.

9. The two boys (*collects, collect*) baseball cards.

10. Since July, Lorenz (*has, have*) painted four pictures.

11. Bradley (*earns, earn*) his blue belt in tae kwon do this year.

12. Dexter and Paul (*enjoys, enjoy*) our school carnivals.

13. The band from Mexico City (*plays, play*) for us frequently.

14. The Herb Show (*has, have*) many interesting booths.

15. Next week, business leaders (*is, are*) hosting a job fair.

INTERVENING PHRASES

5c **The number of the subject is not changed by a phrase following the subject.**

Remember that a verb agrees in number with its subject. The subject is never part of a prepositional phrase.

EXAMPLES   That **curtain** behind the actors **is** new. [The verb *is* agrees with the subject *curtain*.]

The **books** on that shelf **are** dictionaries. [The verb *are* agrees with the subject *books*.]

Compound prepositions such as *together with, in addition to, as well as*, and *along with* following the subject do not affect the number of the subject.

EXAMPLES   **Leona,** as well as her parents, **is** visiting us.

The **lettuce,** in addition to the tomatoes, **has** been washed.

EXERCISE 3   Identifying Subjects and Verbs That Agree in Number

In each of the following sentences, underline the verb form that agrees with the subject. Then underline the subject twice.

EX. 1.   Several <u>cars</u> in the parking lot (*needs,* <u>*need*</u>) washing.

1. A pattern of changing colors (*appears, appear*) on the screen when the computer is not in use.

2. The people from our town (*is, are*) celebrating Nisei Week.

3. The actor, in addition to the producers, (*calls, call*) the daily meetings.

4. The pedestrians in this city (*hears, hear*) the muezzin every day.

5. Two students, together with their teacher, (*is, are*) collecting blankets for flood victims.

6. The signature below the printed name (*was, were*) difficult to read.

7. Ben, as well as Aunt Elaine, (*makes, make*) good couscous.

8. The keys on this keyboard (*feels, feel*) sticky.

9. A huge bouquet of flowers (*was, were*) delivered to my mother.

10. The twins, together with Duane, (*is, are*) taking the bus.

11. Roberto Garcia, Jr., a bronze sculptor who lives south of Kingsville, Texas, (*has, have*) an unusual job.

12. All the work on a bronze sculpture (*is, are*) done by Garcia, himself.

13. Bronze, wax, and clay, along with steel, (*is, are*) materials he works with every day.

14. Two clay statues outside his garage (*guards, guard*) his workshop.

15. Sketches, as well as small models, (*makes, make*) up the first step of a new bronze sculpture.

16. A full-size structure of steel and clay (*goes, go*) together next.

17. Mr. Garcia's kiln, at temperatures of about fifteen hundred degrees Fahrenheit, (*melts, melt*) the wax in a mold.

18. The wax between the mold's layers (*drains, drain*) out.

19. Bronze for the statue (*is, are*) poured into the gap left by the drained wax.

20. Welding, along with sandblasting and grinding, almost (*finishes, finish*) the process.

EXERCISE 4   Proofreading a Paragraph for Subject-Verb Agreement

In the paragraph below, draw a line through each verb that does not agree with its subject. Write the correct verb form in the space above the incorrect word.

has
EX. [1] A student in my biology class ~~have~~ an interesting terrarium.

[1] A fish tank, a gift from Pedro's parents, are the container. [2] The plants in it is mostly nonflowering. [3] The moss, as well as the lichens, have spores, not flowers. [4] The mosses near the front comes from the woods near the school. [5] The lichens on the rock is about five years old, according to my biology teacher. [6] The bright red tips on the lichen is partly fungus. [7] One name for the lichens are "British soldiers." [8] In addition to mosses and lichens, a fern thrive in the terrarium. [9] Our teacher, along with us students, want to start a class terrarium. [10] Some students in the class knows where to get a fish tank and some plants.

AGREEMENT WITH INDEFINITE PRONOUNS

Indefinite pronouns are pronouns that do not refer to a specific person or thing.

5d **The following pronouns are singular:** *each, either, neither, one, everyone, everybody, no one, nobody, anyone, anybody, someone, somebody.*

EXAMPLES   **Neither** of the books **is** difficult. [Neither one is difficult.]
                Someone does have the key.

5e **The following pronouns are plural:** *several, few, both, many.*

EXAMPLES   **Several** of the books **are** easy.   **Both have** keys to the house.

5f **The pronouns** *some, all, most, any,* **and** *none* **may be either singular or plural.**

These pronouns are singular when they refer to a singular word and plural when they refer to a plural word.

SINGULAR   **All** of the report **is** factual.
              Most of the lawn **has** been raked.

  PLURAL   **All** of the facts **are** true.
              Most of the leaves **have** been raked.

The words *any* and *none* may be singular even when they refer to a plural word if the speaker is thinking of each item individually. *Any* and *none* are plural only if the speaker is thinking of several items as a group.

EXAMPLES   **None** of the windows **was** broken. [*Not one window* was broken.]
                None of the windows **were** large. [*No windows* were large.]
                Is any of the windows open? [Is *any one window* open?]
                Any of the windows **are** good places for a plant. [*All the windows* are good places for a plant.]

EXERCISE 5   Using Indefinite Pronouns Correctly

On your own paper, use each of the following word groups as a subject in a sentence. Underline the subjects once and the verbs twice in your sentences.

    EX. 1. Most of my homework

         1. *Most of my homework is finished*.

1. Several of my friends
2. Both Nikki and Emilio
3. Everybody in the room
4. Someone from school
5. Neither of the movies
6. Somebody upstairs
7. All of the guitars
8. Everyone at the meeting
9. Many of the puppets
10. Each fish in the tank
11. None of the streams
12. Few among the volunteers
13. Some of Mr. Dodd's pecans
14. Most of the movies
15. Any of the ribbons
16. No one from our office
17. None of the bread
18. Most of her progress
19. Nobody within the class
20. Any of the softball games

EXERCISE 6 Proofreading a Paragraph for Subject-Verb Agreement

Draw a line through each verb that does not agree with its subject. Write the correct verb form in the space above the incorrect word. Some sentences may contain no agreement errors.

EX. [1] One of my term papers ~~are~~ *is* on Hausa proverbs from the people of northern Nigeria and the Sudan.

[1] All of the proverbs I found makes me really think. [2] Neither of these two proverbs are easy to understand: "It is not the eye which understands, but the mind" and "Lack of knowledge is darker than the night." [3] Both proverbs gives insight into how people think. [4] Some proverbs reflects the Hausa way of life. [5] "A chief is like a trash heap where everyone brings his or her rubbish" seems to show us that the Hausa bring their problems to their leader. [6] Someone like that chief have to be very patient, I think. [7] Several proverbs contains words I had to look up in a dictionary. [8] Most of the unfamiliar words are natural objects, such as cowries and groundnuts. [9] No one I know have clearly explained the proverb "It is by traveling softly, softly that you will sleep in a distant place." [10] One of my teachers have suggested that I also read the proverbs of the Ashanti, one of the native peoples of West Africa.

THE COMPOUND SUBJECT

A *compound subject* has two or more nouns or pronouns that are the subject of the same verb.

5g   Subjects joined by *and* usually take a plural verb.

EXAMPLES   **Cao** and **I are** building the model together. [Two people are building the model.]

Light, warmth, and **water act** together. [Three things act together.]

5h   Compound subjects that name only one person or thing take a singular verb.

EXAMPLE   **Red beans** and **rice is** inexpensive and healthful. [*Red beans* and *rice* is one dish.]

5i   Singular subjects joined by *or* or *nor* take a singular verb.

EXAMPLES   **Either Grandfather** or **Julie has** the scissors. [Only one person has the scissors, not both.]

Neither fog nor **rain stops** this train! [Neither one stops the train.]

5j   When a singular subject and a plural subject are joined by *or* or *nor*, the verb agrees with the subject nearer the verb.

ACCEPTABLE   Either the peaches or the **watermelon is** fine for dessert.
Either the watermelon or the **peaches are** fine for dessert.

BETTER   The **peaches are** fine for dessert, and so **is** the **watermelon.**
The **watermelon is** fine for dessert, and the **peaches are,** too.

You can usually avoid such awkward constructions by rewording the sentence so that each subject has its own verb.

EXAMPLE   Either **Darren is** bringing the children to the ceremony, or his mother and **father are.**

EXERCISE 7   Choosing Verbs That Agree in Number with Their Subjects

In each of the following sentences, underline the correct form of the verb in parentheses.

EX. 1. Charles and Pang (*is, are*) on the team.

1. Either the tuba or the saxophones (*plays, play*) first.

2. Neither my mother nor my father (*is, are*) eager to go.

3. Either Yori or Sheila (*has, have*) extra flyers.

4. Macaroni and cheese (*is, are*) our favorite food.

5. The audience and the actors (*likes, like*) that play.

6. Ariel Sharon and Ehud Barak (*was, were*) prime ministers of Israel.

7. Either Jun or Asa (*has, have*) time to saw the boards.

8. Blocks and a drum (*is, are*) all a two-year-old child needs for entertainment.

9. Neither pencil and paper nor a calculator (*was, were*) available.

10. Rock-and-roll always (*catches, catch*) my sister's attention.

11. Jordan's sketch and Meg's painting (*was, were*) finished.

12. My brother and sister never (*enjoys, enjoy*) arguing.

13. Tents, backpacks, and food (*has, have*) been packed.

14. Neither the pharmacy nor the front desk (*is, are*) answering.

15. (*Was, Were*) chicken and dumplings on the menu today?

16. Both salsa and gazpacho (*requires, require*) tomatoes as ingredients.

17. Patricia, Susan, and Guy (*works, work*) well together.

18. Scissors and paper (*does, do*) need to be on the list.

19. Paula, her brothers, and her sister (*wishes, wish*) to help Mrs. Landowski.

20. Either Mrs. Columbo or Mr. Andrews (*is, are*) able to help them, too.

21. Pencil or pens (*writes, write*) equally well on this type of paper.

22. Bonnie and Rolando (*has, have*) agreed to run for office.

23. How soon (*is, are*) Etta and Albert leaving on vacation?

24. Mark and Coretta (*watches, watch*) the runners carefully.

25. (*Does, Do*) Erica or Han-Ling cast the last vote?

MODULE 5: AGREEMENT
DOESN'T / DON'T AND COLLECTIVE NOUNS

5k   ***Don't*** **and** ***doesn't*** **must agree with their subjects.**

Contractions are two words combined into one, with one or more letters omitted. *Don't* is the contraction for *do not*. *Doesn't* is the contraction for *does not*.

With the subjects *I* and *you* and with plural subjects, use *don't* (*do not*).

EXAMPLES   I **don't** see anything.   They **don't** care.
              You **don't** need one.   Sales **don't** last long.

With other singular subjects, use the singular *doesn't* (*does not*).

EXAMPLES   He **doesn't** work here.   The sweater **doesn't** fit.
              This **doesn't** look hard.   Lily **doesn't** feel sick.

5l   **Collective nouns may be either singular or plural.**

Collective nouns are singular in form, but they name a *group* of persons or things.

Collective Nouns		
army	committee	herd
assembly	family	jury
audience	fleet	public
class	flock	swarm
club	group	team

Use a plural verb with a collective noun when you refer to the individual parts or members of the group acting separately. Use a singular verb when you refer to the group acting together as a unit.

EXAMPLES   The **jury have** not been home yet. [*Jury* is thought of as individuals.]
              The **jury has** finally reached a verdict. [*Jury* is thought of as a unit.]

EXERCISE 8   Using *Doesn't* and *Don't* Correctly

Use *doesn't* or *don't* correctly to complete each sentence below.

EX. 1. I ___*don't*___ need help with this.

1. We _____ serve any Moroccan food here.

2. _____ you serve couscous?

3. Well, our dish _____ contain meat.

4. You _____ need to use lamb, but it adds good flavor.

5. These recipes _____ require a special steamer.

6. The supermarket _____ sell lamb broth.

7. _____ Jolon need more chickpeas?

8. The vegetables _____ need a separate bowl.

9. It _____ look hard to make.

10. _____ this taste delicious!

11. Some newspapers _____ have many recipes like this.

12. _____ you grow some of these vegetables?

13. Herbs _____ seem to be difficult to grow.

14. Preparing the garden _____ take long.

15. _____ overwater the herbs and vegetables.

EXERCISE 9   Writing Sentences with Collective Nouns

Select five collective nouns from the chart on the preceding page. On your own paper, write a pair of sentences using each noun. Each pair of sentences should show how the collective noun may be either singular or plural.

EX. 1. *The swarm is huge!*

     1. *The swarm are flying in different directions.*

5m   A verb agrees with its subject, not with its predicate nominative.

EXAMPLES
$$\text{S} \quad \text{V} \qquad\qquad \text{P.N.}$$
The **prize is** two concert tickets.
$$\qquad\qquad\quad \text{S} \qquad \text{V} \quad \text{P.N.}$$
Two concert **tickets are** the prize.

5n   When the subject follows the verb, find the subject and make sure that the verb agrees with it.

The most common cases in which the subject follows the verb are in questions and in sentences beginning with *here* or *there*.

EXAMPLES   Here **is** a **menorah.**
Here **are** some **candles.**

There **is** a new **student** in class.
There **are** new **students** in class.

Does the **map** show this road?
Do these **roads** appear on the map?

5o   Words stating an amount are usually singular.

EXAMPLES   **Six dollars is** a lot for that.
Your **five minutes is** up.

Sometimes, however, the amount is thought of as individual pieces or parts. If so, a plural verb is used.

EXAMPLES   **Two** of the dollars **are** silver dollars.
Three fourths of the pencils **are** sharpened.

5p   *Every* or *many a* before a subject calls for a singular verb.

EXAMPLES   **Every** shelf **has** a kachina doll on it.
Many a doll **was** made of cottonwood root.

5q   A few nouns, although plural in form, take singular verbs.

EXAMPLES   The **news is** grim this week.
Unfortunately, **measles is** showing up in young adults.

NOTE   Some nouns that end in *–s* take a plural verb even though they refer to a single item.
     EXAMPLES   The **scissors are** on the table.
              Your **pants are** clean.

EXERCISE 10 Identifying Subjects and Verbs That Agree in Number

In each sentence below, underline the verb form that agrees with the subject. Then underline the subject twice.

EX. 1. A relay <u>team</u> (<u>*is*</u>, *are*) three people.

1. Eight miles (*is*, *are*) a long race.

2. Two different prizes (*was*, *were*) given at the party.

3. Many a trophy (*has*, *have*) been won by that team!

4. Politics (*determines*, *determine*) the choice of team captain.

5. (*Does*, *Do*) Ulani have the same coach?

6. The winner (*is*, *are*) the first-year runners.

7. There (*is*, *are*) professional recruiters in the bleachers today.

8. Every race (*has*, *have*) a clear favorite.

9. Here (*is*, *are*) the name of the best runner.

10. Many unknown runners (*has*, *have*) won the steeplechase.

11. (*Does*, *Do*) Gisela have a good chance of winning in the next race?

12. Where (*is*, *are*) your friend Rudy now?

13. That relay team always (*goes*, *go*) on to the regional meet.

14. Every heat (*has*, *have*) six runners in it.

15. The shorts with green and while stripes (*is*, *are*) Emilio's.

16. Why (*does*, *do*) Caron and Aponte always get here early?

17. Twenty minutes (*has*, *have*) passed since the starting gun went off.

18. Five kilometers (*is*, *are*) the distance of the cross-country race.

19. Three of those kilometers (*leads*, *lead*) up steep hills.

20. Tonight the news (*covers*, *cover*) some of the races.

21. Here (*is*, *are*) the books you were looking for.

22. Few varieties of oak tree (*grows*, *grow*) in our state.

23. (*Hasn't*, *Haven't*) Andrés passed his driving test?

24. Gayle's trousers (*is*, *are*) a dark shade of green.

25. There (*is*, *are*) a new family on our block.

MODULE 5: AGREEMENT

REVIEW EXERCISE

A. Choosing Verbs That Agree in Number with Their Subjects

In each of the sentences below, underline the correct form of the verb in parentheses.

EX. 1. The men in the picture (*is, are*) artists.

1. Each (*has, have*) a brush, some black ink, and a sheet of paper.

2. (*Does, Do*) your sister use a camel's hair brush?

3. The audience (*likes, like*) the bamboo with the drooping leaves.

4. Many in the room (*enjoys, enjoy*) painting.

5. (*Does, Do*) the artists often make their own inks?

6. The ink, the brush, and the silk (*affects, affect*) the finish of a painting done on silk.

7. Either Mr. Tsai or his teacher (*is, are*) demonstrating different kinds of brush strokes.

8. Where (*is, are*) the scrolls that contain all the writing?

9. Neither the words nor the drawing (*is, are*) red.

10. Forty dollars (*seems, seem*) reasonable to me.

11. You (*wasn't, weren't*) home when we telephoned.

12. One of the articles (*is, are*) about N. Scott Momaday.

13. We (*was, were*) talking about these machines in French class.

14. Nobody in these stores (*sells, sell*) my kind of shoe.

15. (*Does, Do*) apples and oranges come in the next shipment?

16. Each of the contestants (*seems, seem*) pleased with the judges' final decision.

17. Theo, Jerry, and Ed (*wants, want*) to work for you.

18. Jeanine and her parents (*gets, get*) all of the mail.

19. Either Gloria or Sandra (*has, have*) a watch with a second hand.

20. The effects of the long dry spell (*was, were*) deadly for crops and cattle.

B. Proofreading a Paragraph for Subject-Verb Agreement

In the sentences below, draw a line through each verb that does not agree with its subject. Write the correct verb form in the space above the incorrect word. Some sentences have no errors in subject-verb agreement.

EX. [1] One of my cousins ~~are~~ *is* a great collector.

[1] The news are full of stories about lucky breaks. [2] You might read about how somebody find a rare book in an attic. [3] Few of these stories is completely true. [4] Still, my cousin and I like to hear them. [5] We has spent many weekends going to yard sales. [6] There is often collections of baseball cards for sale. [7] These sales offers a great opportunity for collectors. [8] People often don't know which cards are special. [9] Several of the older cards has greater value today than ever before. [10] The cards in my collection was made before 1960.

C. Writing Trivia Questions

Your job as a copywriter is to write questions for a television trivia game show. Your category for the next program is the Olympics. Use reference books, magazines, or encyclopedias to learn some details about the Olympics. Then, on your own paper, create fifteen questions from your notes. Underline the subjects once and the verbs twice in your questions, and make sure they agree.

EX. Notes: *games held in Olympia, Greece, every four years between 776 B.C. and A.D. 393*

Question: *Where were the first games held?*

MODULE 5: AGREEMENT

PRONOUN-ANTECEDENT AGREEMENT

A pronoun usually refers to a noun or another pronoun that comes before it. The word that a pronoun refers to is called its *antecedent*.

5r   A pronoun should agree with its antecedent in number and gender.

Some singular personal pronouns have forms that indicate the gender of the antecedent. Masculine pronouns (*he, him, his*) refer to males. Feminine pronouns (*she, her, hers*) refer to females. Neuter pronouns (*it, its*) refer to things that are neither male nor female, and often to animals.

EXAMPLES   **Sean** took **his** calculator with **him.**
                       Mrs. Torres said that **she** would share **her** lunch.
                       The **trunk** is missing **its** key.

The gender of other pronouns is determined by the phrase that follows the pronoun.

EXAMPLES   **Neither** of the **women** forgot **her** lines. [*Women*, in the phrase that
                       follows *Neither*, determines the pronoun's gender.]
                       One **person** left **her** or **his** scarf. [*Person* could be either masculine or
                       feminine.]

(1) Use a singular pronoun to refer to *each, either, neither, one, everyone, everybody, no one, nobody, anyone, anybody, someone,* or *somebody.*

EXAMPLES   **Each** cast **his** or **her** vote.
                       One of the striped socks lost **its** mate.

(2) Use a singluar pronoun to refer to two or more singular antecedents joined by *or* or *nor*.

EXAMPLES   Either **Lucia** or **Marna** will explain **her** experiment.
                       Neither my **father** nor **Rudy** brought **his** camera.

(3) Two or more antecedents joined by and should be referred to by a plural pronoun.

EXAMPLES   **Lionel** and **Laura** were proud of **their** son.
                       Mr. Tower, Todd, and **I** will do **our** best.

EXERCISE 11   Identifying Antecedents and Writing Pronouns

On the line in each sentence below, write a pronoun that agrees with its antecedent. Underline the antecedent.

EX. 1. <u>Mr. Sharp</u> offered _____*his*_____ opinion.

1. No one in the party had forgotten _____ ticket.

2. For many people, this trip to the jungle was _____ first.

3. Flora always carried _____ camera.

4. The train stopped four times on _____ way to the plantation.

5. Neither my sister nor Hazel needed _____ snacks.

6. At the many stops, local people sold _____ goods.

7. One person left _____ hat on the seat.

8. Toshiro and Greg struggled to get _____ seats by the window.

9. The banana plantation ships much of _____ fruit to other countries.

10. One of the men brought _____ puppy on the train.

11. Tara took _____ lamb to the county fair.

12. Our town had _____ centennial celebration last week.

13. Renaldo and Kazuo always go to _____ gymnastic classes.

14. Either Nora or Rosa will invite _____ mother to the open house.

15. Both of the boys went to _____ extra practices to prepare for the Olympic trials.

16. The new motor scooter received _____ first dent.

17. Nobody in our family forgets to wear _____ seat belt when riding in the car.

18. The truck and bicycle had mud all over _____ wheels.

19. Wendy decided that _____ could meet us after all.

20. Did Dr. Bryan agree that she should make _____ speech for our health class?

MODULE REVIEW

A. Proofreading Sentences for Subject-Verb and Pronoun-Antecedent Agreement

For each error in agreement in the following sentences, draw a line through the incorrect word, and write the correct form above it. If the sentence is correct, write C.

EX. _____ 1. Politics *is* ~~are~~ not as interesting as science.

_____ 1. Where are your report on meteorites?

_____ 2. The students in the front row hears Ms. Swift better than I do.

_____ 3. Somebody in my class forgot to write their name on a paper.

_____ 4. The chart is actually several different photographs put together.

_____ 5. Neither Nancy nor Yolanda want to give their report.

_____ 6. Every comet were seen as an omen of things to come.

_____ 7. Few of my classmates has ever seen an aerial photograph of our city.

_____ 8. Fifteen minutes are a long time to talk!

_____ 9. Do each of the boys want some of this salad?

_____ 10. Each of the women presented their findings separately.

_____ 11. Lori and Yoko, besides arriving early, has brought our dessert.

_____ 12. Many of us agree that Robert Frost is one of America's greatest poets.

_____ 13. Several of my classmates is going to the amusement park today.

_____ 14. Have any of the group members brought the paper and paint for the banners?

_____ 15. Some of the father's answers to his son's questions is funny.

_____ 16. Room and board is included in the summer camp fee.

_____ 17. The garden don't take as much work as I thought it would.

_____ 18. Which questions on the test is hardest for you?

_____ 19. At noon, the posse are leaving to begin the search.

_____ 20. There is twenty students in my Chemistry I class.

B. Proofreading a Paragraph for Subject-Verb and Pronoun-Antecedent Agreement

In the paragraph below, draw a line through each incorrect verb or pronoun. Write the correct form in the space above the incorrect word. Some sentences have no errors in agreement.

EX. [1] There *is* many people in my family.
(*are* written above *is*)

[1] My entire family visit Nara every summer. [2] Everybody look forward to this trip. [3] My father and grandfather always plays *Go* for one evening. [4] Neither my mother nor my grandmother enjoy the game. [5] She both prefer to walk though the streets of Nara. [6] During the day we all likes to wander in the park. [7] Each of us has their favorite part of the park. [8] Grandfather and Grandmother always spends an hour or two at the statue of Buddha. [9] The most interesting part for me are all the people from many nations. [10] Everyone in the family tries to guess a person's home country.

C. Writing a Letter to a Pen Pal

After waiting many months, you have finally learned the name and address of your new pen pal. On your own paper, make notes about things you might want this person to know about you. You might tell about your family, your birthday, your age, and what grade you are in. Your new friend might like to know your favorite food, movie, sport, color, or holiday. Use your notes to write ten sentences in a letter to introduce yourself to your pen pal. Be sure to put your address in your letter so your new friend will know where to mail his or her answer. In your sentences, check that your verbs agree with their subjects and that your pronouns agree with their antecedents.

EX.

> *Mara Aboud*
> *1573 Orangewood Pl.*
> *Grants Pass, OR 97526*

> *Dear Lani,*
> *My name is Mara, and I'd like to be your new pen pal. I'll tell you about myself.*

REGULAR VERBS

6a The four principal parts of a verb are the *base form*, the *present participle*, the *past*, and the *past participle*.

EXAMPLES   We **walk** to school. [base form of *walk*]
We are **walking** home. [present participle of *walk*]
We **walked** to the store. [past of *walk*]
We have **walked** for hours. [past participle of *walk*]

Notice that the tenses made from the present participle and past participle use helping verbs, such as *am, is, are, has,* and *have.*

6b A *regular verb* is a verb that forms its past and past participle by adding *–d* or *–ed* to the base form.

Base Form	Present Participle	Past	Past Participle
happen	(is) happening	happened	(have) happened
create	(is) creating	created	(have) created
carry	(is) carrying	carried	(have) carried

The present participle of most regular verbs ending in *–e* drops the *–e* before adding *–ing*.

NOTE   A few regular verbs have an alternate past form ending in *–t*. For example, the past form of *burn* is *burned* or *burnt*.

EXERCISE 1   Writing the Correct Forms of Regular Verbs

For each of the following sentences, decide what the correct form of the italicized verb should be. Write the correct verb form on the line in the sentence.

EX.   1. Last night's train (*arrive*) _____*arrived*_____ on time.

1. Ashur has (*admit*) _____ that he forgot the flowers.

2. Before she left, Lien (*pledge*) _____ to return.

3. Yes, we have (*create*) _____ a new gumbo.

4. My sister, who loves gardening, is (*plant*) _____ both fruits and vegetables.

5. Although we (*hurry*) _____, we missed the bus.

6. During World War II, hundreds of Navajos in the U.S. Marines (*work*)

    _____ as Code Talkers.

7. The club members are (*urge*) _____ us to join.

8. What has (*happen*) _____ to that building?

9. The method that Thelma is (*use*) _____ was developed in India.

10. Yesterday morning the class (*watch*) _____ a film about pollution.

11. The rest of the workers have (*decide*) _____ to follow my suggestion.

12. Every morning last month we (*listen*) _____ to a weather report.

13. Ms. Perkins has (*correct*) _____ the errors.

14. I think that dog is (*follow*) _____ us!

15. The radio station (*play*) _____ my two favorite songs last night.

16. Our neighbor down the street is (*move*) _____ to another town.

17. I (*promise*) _____ that I would feed the cat every morning.

18. Sheila (*search*) _____ for hours, but she could not find her keys.

19. Our art class is (*visit*) _____ the museum today.

20. Because the fans have (*wait*) _____ for a long time, they are getting restless.

IRREGULAR VERBS

6c   An *irregular verb* is a verb that forms its past and past participle in some other way than by adding *–d* or *–ed* to the base form.

Irregular verbs form their past and past participle by changing vowels, changing consonants, adding *–en*, or making no change at all.

Base Form	Past	Past participle
begin	began	(have) begun
go	went	(have) gone
take	took	(have) taken
set	set	(have) set

Since most English verbs are regular, people sometimes try to make irregular verbs follow the same pattern. However, words such as *knowed* and *thinked* are considered nonstandard. If you are not sure about the parts of a verb, look in a dictionary which lists the principal parts of irregular verbs.

When the present participle and past participle forms are used as main verbs (simple predicates) in sentences, they always require helping verbs.

Present Participle + Helping Verb = Verb Phrase			
running		forms	am running
driving	+	of	= was driving
seeing		*be*	were seeing

Past Participle + Helping Verb = Verb Phrase			
run		forms	have run
driven	+	of	= has driven
seen		*have*	had seen

IRREGULAR VERBS FREQUENTLY MISUSED

Base Form	Present Participle	Past	Past Participle
begin	(is) beginning	began	(have) begun
blow	(is) blowing	blew	(have) blown
break	(is) breaking	broke	(have) broken
bring	(is) bringing	brought	(have) brought
burst	(is) bursting	burst	(have) burst
choose	(is) choosing	chose	(have) chosen
come	(is) coming	came	(have) come
dive	(is) diving	dove (*or* dived)	(have) dived
do	(is) doing	did	(have) done
drink	(is) drinking	drank	(have) drunk
drive	(is) driving	drove	(have) driven
eat	(is) eating	ate	(have) eaten
fall	(is) falling	fell	(have) fallen
freeze	(is) freezing	froze	(have) frozen
give	(is) giving	gave	(have) given
go	(is) going	went	(have) gone
grow	(is) growing	grew	(have) grown
know	(is) knowing	knew	(have) known
make	(is) making	made	(have) made
put	(is) putting	put	(have) put
ride	(is) riding	rode	(have) ridden
ring	(is) ringing	rang	(have) rung
run	(is) running	ran	(have) run
see	(is) seeing	saw	(have) seen
shake	(is) shaking	shook	(have) shaken
shrink	(is) shrinking	shrank (*or* shrunk)	(have) shrunk
sink	(is) sinking	sank	(have) sunk
speak	(is) speaking	spoke	(have) spoken
steal	(is) stealing	stole	(have) stolen
sting	(is) stinging	stung	(have) stung

IRREGULAR VERBS FREQUENTLY MISUSED			
Base Form	**Present Participle**	**Past**	**Past Participle**
strike	(is) striking	struck	(have) struck
swear	(is) swearing	swore	(have) sworn
swim	(is) swimming	swam	(have) swum
take	(is) taking	took	(have) taken
tear	(is) tearing	tore	(have) torn
throw	(is) throwing	threw	(have) thrown
wear	(is) wearing	wore	(have) worn
write	(is) writing	wrote	(have) written

EXERCISE 2   Writing Forms of Irregular Verbs

Change each of the verb forms below. If the base form is given, change it to the present participle. If the present participle is given, change it to the past form. If the past form is given, change it to the past participle. Use *have* before the past participle form and *is* before the present participle form.

EX.   1. is diving _____*dove*_____   2. ran ____*have run*____

1. see _____

2. spoke _____

3. is freezing _____

4. threw _____

5. is breaking _____

6. brought _____

7. grow _____

8. drove _____

9. is swimming _____

10. began _____

11. speak _____

12. is choosing _____

13. wear _____

14. knew _____

15. ride _____

16. shook _____

17. is eating _____

18. went _____

19. take _____

20. drank _____

EXERCISE 3   Identifying Correct Forms of Irregular Verbs

For each of the following sentences, underline the correct form of the verb in parentheses.

EX. 1. Those plants have (*grew, grown*) taller.

1. The class (*chose, chosen*) new officers last week.

2. Did you know your rear axle has (*broke, broken*)?

3. An earthquake (*struck, strike*) Antigua earlier today.

4. I'm afraid your sweater (*shrank, shrunk*) in the wash.

5. About four inches of rain has (*fell, fallen*) since yesterday.

6. Anica angrily (*tore, torn*) the letter into bits.

7. My grandfather has (*wrote, written*) several articles for *National Geographic*.

8. You can try after Rudy has (*dove, dived*) off the board.

9. The concert has (*began, begun*), but you have not missed much.

10. Mr. Katz (*shaken, shook*) his head in reply.

EXERCISE 4   Proofreading a Paragraph for Correct Verb Forms

Proofread the paragraph below. If a sentence contains an incorrect verb form, draw a line through the wrong form and write the correct form above it. Some sentences may have no errors in verb forms.

saw
EX.   1.   Last year we ~~seen~~ some of the studios in Bombay.

[1] The film industry in India has grew tremendously. [2] Today India's film industry was the largest in the world. [3] Since 1979, India has made more than seven hundred films each year! [4] Only lately have I began to notice the number of Indian films. [5] I had went to an Indian film festival to see a film by Satyajit Ray. [6] I seen several others while I was there. [7] When one film began, I recognized the lead actor. [8] I could have swore that he was in two other films at the same festival. [9] Later, I done a little research on him. [10] He had maked more than a dozen films that year.

EXERCISE 5   Using Irregular Verbs

On your own paper, write fifteen sentences using verbs from the charts on module section 7c. Use the participle forms of the verbs in five of your sentences. Underline the verbs you use.

EX.   1.   Frederick <u>has brought</u> us a bushel of potatoes.

6d   **The time expressed by a verb is called the *tense* of the verb.**

Every verb in English has six tenses.

Tense	Examples
Present	I throw, you throw, he throws, we throw
Past	I threw, you threw, she threw, they threw
Future	I will (shall) throw, you will throw, they will throw
Present Perfect	I have thrown, you have thrown, he has thrown
Past Perfect	I had thrown, you had thrown, she had thrown
Future Perfect	I will (shall) have thrown, you will have thrown, we will have thrown

Each of the six tenses has an additional form, called the ***progressive form,*** which expresses a continuing action. It consists of a form of the verb *be* plus the present participle of a verb. The progressive is not a separate tense but an additional form of each of the six tenses.

Form	Examples
Present Progressive	am/are/is throwing
Past Progressive	was/were throwing
Future Progressive	will (shall) be throwing
Present Perfect Progressive	has/have been throwing
Past Perfect Progressive	had been throwing
Future Perfect Progressive	will (shall) have been throwing

6e   **Do not change needlessly from one tense to another.**

NONSTANDARD   Elia drove to the store and buys lunch. [*Drove* is past tense; *buys* is present tense.]

STANDARD   Elia **drove** to the store and **bought** lunch. [*Drove* and *bought* are both past tense.]

EXERCISE 6   Identifying Verb Tenses

For each sentence below, identify the tense of the verb. Write your answers on your own paper.

EX.   1.   Kam had seen the movie.
       1.   *past perfect*

1.   The team traveled by bus.
2.   Leila has taken her medicine.
3.   The conference will begin on Monday.
4.   We swim on Friday evenings.
5.   Phillip had already seen the movie.

EXERCISE 7   Proofreading a Paragraph for Consistent Verb Tenses

Decide whether the paragraph below should be written in the present or past tense. Then draw a line through each incorrect verb form, and write the correct form above it.

            ate
EX.   [1]   I ~~eat~~ too quickly, so I got these hiccups.

[1] Most times, hiccups are not dangerous, but they are a nuisance. [2] Also; most people found them funny. [3] Yesterday, my hiccups continue for a while, so my friends gave me advice. [4] Maripat tells me to hold my breath and count to ten. [5] Shing says that I should quickly drink a tall glass of water. [6] Other people suggest ideas that sound really strange. [7] My mother says that I should put a pail or a wastebasket over my head and have someone beat on it. [8] My sister gave me the best idea of all. [9] She went into the kitchen and comes back with a paper bag. [10] I place it over my head, and my hiccups vanished.

EXERCISE 8   Using Verb Tenses and Forms Correctly

On your own paper, write five sentences showing the correct use of the verb *bring*. Use as many different verb tenses and forms as you can. Underline each verb, and label its tense or form.

EX.   1.   *Dad is bringing my sister Leta to watch my game. (present progressive)*

ACTIVE AND PASSIVE VOICE

6f **A verb in the *active voice* expresses an action done *by* its subject. A verb in the *passive voice* expresses an action done *to* its subject.**

ACTIVE VOICE   Mr. Noor **helped** Sarah. [The subject, *Mr. Noor*, performed the action.]

PASSIVE VOICE   Sarah **was helped** by Mr. Noor. [The subject, *Sarah*, received the action.]

NOTE   In a passive sentence, the verb phrase always includes a form of *be* and the past participle of the main verb. Other helping verbs may also be included.

The passive voice emphasizes the person or thing receiving the action. It may be used when the speaker does not know or does not wish to say who performed the action.

               SUBJECT

PASSIVE VOICE   A window **was broken** by someone last night.

               SUBJECT   OBJECT

ACTIVE VOICE   Someone **broke** a window last night.

In general, you should avoid using the passive voice because it makes your writing sound weak and awkward. Using the active voice helps make your writing direct and forceful.

EXERCISE 9   Classifying Sentences by Voice

Identify each of the following sentences as active or passive. On the line before each sentence, write *act.* for *active* or *pass.* for *passive.*

EX.   _____*act.*_____   1.   Pat Cummings illustrates books.

_____   1.   She has been inspired by Tom Feelings.

_____   2.   Her work is created in Brooklyn.

_____   3.   Cummings uses a variety of materials in her work.

_____   4.   *Jimmy Lee Did It* was illustrated by Cummings.

_____   5.   Our school library owns several of her books.

_____   6.   My sister can be counted among her first big fans.

_____   7.   Sarita was surprised by the invitation.

_____   8.   Was Pat Cummings asked by the art teacher to visit our school?

_____ 9. Did she ever really come?

_____ 10. The program was enjoyed by all of us.

_____ 11. I hope we get more programs.

_____ 12. How many books were suggested?

_____ 13. Wynona reads several books each month.

_____ 14. Our teacher wants us to form a book club.

_____ 15. Did she give you any ideas for a club name?

MODULE 6: USING VERBS CORRECTLY

LIE *AND* LAY

6g The verb *lie* means "to rest," "to recline," or "to remain in a lying position." *Lie* rarely takes an object. The verb *lay* means "to put" or "to place" (something). *Lay* usually takes an object.

EXAMPLES   The dog **is lying** in the doorway.

Sarah **lay** the mat in front of the door.

PRINCIPAL PARTS OF *LIE* AND *LAY*			
Base Form	**Present Participle**	**Past**	**Past Participle**
lie (to recline)	(is) lying	lay	(have) lain
lay (to put)	(is) laying	laid	(have) laid

NOTE   The verb *lie* may be used to describe the lying position of inanimate objects as well as of people and animals. Even though someone puts an object down, it *lies* (not *lays*) there.

EXAMPLE   Your book **is lying** on the table.

When deciding whether to use *lie* or *lay*, ask yourself two questions.

QUESTION 1:   What do I want to say? Is the meaning "to be in a lying position," or is it "to put something down"?

QUESTION 2:   What time does the verb express, and which principal part is used to show this time?

The following examples show how you can apply these questions to determine which verb—*lie* or *lay*—should be used.

EXAMPLE   That blanket has always (*lain, laid*) on the back of the couch.

QUESTION 1:   Meaning? The meaning is "to be in a lying position." Therefore, the verb should be *lie.*

QUESTION 2:   Principal part? The verb expresses the past, and the sentence requires the past participle with *has.* The past participle of *lie* is *lain.*

ANSWER: That blanket **has** always **lain** on the back of the couch.

EXERCISE 10   Choosing the Correct Forms of *Lie* and *Lay*

For each of the following sentences, underline the correct form of *lie* or *lay*.

EX.   1. The mummy had (*laid, lain*) in the ground for centuries.

1. Early Egyptians sometimes (*laid, lay*) bodies in dry sand.

2. Other mummies have been (*lying, laying*) in frozen earth for hundreds of years.

3. About 2,100 years ago, someone in Hunan, China, had (*lain, laid*) the body of a woman in a burial mound.

4. The mummy (*laid, lay*) there until the Chinese government decided to build a hospital on that site.

5. Native Americans sometimes (*laid, lay*) bodies inside dry caves.

6. One such mummy had (*lain, laid*) in a Kentucky cave for two thousand years.

7. Egyptian embalmers (*lain, laid*) strips of linen over their dead.

8. Often, a person's organs (*lay, laid*) inside a separate jar.

9. The friends of John Paul Jones (*lain, laid*) his body in a lead casket that was full of alcohol.

10. His mummy had (*lain, laid*) there for over one hundred years.

11. Instead of (*lying, laying*) down, some mummies are put in a seated position.

12. Did you know that Egyptian mummies at one point in the process (*lay, laid*) in sodium carbonate?

13. Before being (*laid, lain*) in a tomb, mummies were given a treatment lasting seventy days.

14. The body of King Mer-en-re was found (*lying, laying*) in a tomb in 1880.

15. Besides the mummy, articles from a person's life were (*laid, lain*) in the tomb.

EXERCISE 11   Using *Lie* and *Lay* Correctly

On your own paper, write five sentences using the different forms of *lie* correctly. Then write five sentences using the different forms of *lay* correctly. Use all of the principal parts at least once in your sentences. Underline and label all the forms of *lie* and *lay* in your sentences.

EX.   1. *Chandra laid her pen beside her book.* (*past*)

MODULE 6: USING VERBS CORRECTLY

SIT *AND* SET *AND* RISE *AND* RAISE

SIT AND *SET*

6h The verb *sit* means "to rest in an upright, seated position." *Sit* almost never takes an object. The verb *set* means "to put" or "to place" (something). *Set* usually takes an object. Notice that *set* does not change form in the past or past participle.

PRINCIPAL PARTS OF *SIT* AND *SET*			
Base Form	**Present Participle**	**Past**	**Past Participle**
sit (to rest)	(is) sitting	sat	(have) sat
set (to put)	(is) setting	set	(have) set

EXAMPLES   **Sit** here.   **Set** your end down first.
                 The box **sat** on the table.   The driver **set** it there.

EXERCISE 12 Using the Forms of *Sit* and *Set*

In each of the following sentences, write the correct form of *sit* or *set* on the line provided.

EX.   1. Thi and I will both _____*sit*_____ in the back seat.

1. Thi has _____ a pad of paper between us.

2. When I _____ down, I felt a pencil on the seat.

3. We _____ on the floor playing word games and talking about school.

4. Don't _____ your lunch box on the window ledge, or your food will spoil.

5. When the car stopped, I _____ our picnic basket on the table.

6. Thi was reading about Lewis Carroll, but she _____ the book down.

7. We have _____ here for an hour playing *Mischmasch*, one of Carroll's games.

8. I wrote the letters "HTH" on the page and then _____ the pencil beside me.

9. Thi _____ for a long time, trying to think of a word containing that letter combination.

10. When we _____ at lunch the next day, I whispered, "Lighthouse."

RISE AND RAISE

6i **The verb *rise* means "to go in an upward direction." *Rise* rarely takes an object. The verb *raise* means "to move something in an upward direction." *Raise* usually takes an object.**

PRINCIPAL PARTS OF *RISE* AND *RAISE*			
Base Form	**Present Participle**	**Past**	**Past Participle**
rise (to go up)	(is) rising	rose	(have) risen
raise (to move something up)	(is) raising	raised	(have) raised

EXAMPLES   My parents **rise** at about 6:30 most mornings.
I'm glad you **raised** that issue!
The price of oranges will **rise** again.
The store **raised** the price of its fruit.

EXERCISE 13   Using the Forms of *Rise* and *Raise*

Write the correct form of *rise* or *raise* on the line in each sentence below.

EX.   1. If you add yeast, the dough will _____*rise*_____.

1. Matzo contains no yeast, so the dough does not _____.

2. My aunt _____ at dawn to start her bread.

3. She has _____ earlier than usual.

4. At dinner, my uncle _____ the napkin and peeked underneath.

5. Before a particularly good dessert, everyone's excitement will

   _____.

MODULE REVIEW

A. Writing Sentences Using the Correct Forms of Verbs

On your own paper, write twenty sentences using the following verbs.

EX. 1. sunk
    1. *The raft had sunk last summer.*

1.	laid	11.	froze
2.	(have) walked	12.	(have) shaken
3.	seen	13.	(is) bringing
4.	swam	14.	stole
5.	(had) set	15.	stung
6.	lying	16.	(have) chosen
7.	rose	17.	raise
8.	thrown	18.	began
9.	drove	19.	(have) given
10.	(had) used	20.	(is) doing

B. Proofreading a Paragraph for Correct Verb Forms

In the following paragraph, if a sentence contains an incorrect verb form, cross out the incorrect verb. Then write the correct form above the verb. Some sentences will be correct. Others may have more than one incorrect verb form.

began

EX. [1] Cochise and Thomas Jeffords ~~beginned~~ a long friendship.

[1] In the late 1800s, the Apache leader Cochise was arrest on a false charge.

[2] He escaped and later striked back at the settlers. [3] At one point, his people had killed

more than a dozen mail carriers. [4] Thomas Jeffords, the man in charge of the mail,

decides to visit Cochise. [5] When they met, he sets his own weapons aside.

[6] Then the two men set and talked for days. [7] After this meeting, the men had became

good friends, and Jeffords was chose to be the agent for the Apache reservation. [8] The

men's friendship lasted until the chief's death in 1874. [9] Shortly thereafter, Jeffords was

replace by a different agent, and a new leader raised to power among the Apaches. [10]

His name, Geronimo, was soon knew throughout the United States.

C.   Writing a Weather Report

You are a weather forecaster on a local television station. For tonight's show, you will be using the weather map that is shown below. When you display the map, you will describe the weather situation to your audience.

1.   First, use the weather symbols to determine what the weather is in different parts of the country.

2.   Next, make notes on your own paper. Write five sentences about the weather. Use each of the following verbs at least once: *sit, lie,* and *rise.*

EX.   1. *A stationary front is sitting over northern Florida.*

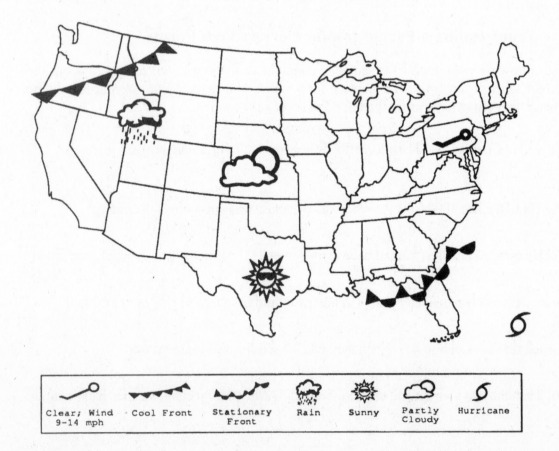

MODULE 7: USING PRONOUNS CORRECTLY

CASE OF PRONOUNS

Case is the form of a noun or pronoun that shows its use in a sentence. In English, there are three cases: *nominative, objective*, and *possessive*.

The form of a noun is the same for the nominative and objective cases.

NOMINATIVE CASE   The **judge** has issued a ruling. [noun used as subject]

OBJECTIVE CASE   I respect the **judge**. [noun used as direct object]

A noun changes its form only in the possessive case, usually by adding an apostrophe and an *s*.

POSSESSIVE CASE   The **judge's** ruling was fair.

Unlike nouns, most personal pronouns have different forms for the nominative, objective, and possessive cases.

PERSONAL PRONOUNS			
	Nominative Case	**Objective Case**	**Possessive Case**
Singular	I you he, she, it	me you him, her, it	my, mine your, yours his, her, hers, its
Plural	we you they	us you them	our, ours your, yours their, theirs

NOTE   Some teachers prefer to call possessive forms of pronouns (such as *hers, your*, and *their*) adjectives. Follow your teacher's instructions regarding possessive forms.

EXERCISE 1   Identifying Personal Pronouns and Their Cases

Identify the case of the italicized pronoun in each sentence below. On the line before each sentence, write *nom.* for *nominative, obj.* for *objective*, or *poss.* for *possessive*.

EX.   *poss.*   1. Benito Pablo Juárez earned *his* place in history as one of the greatest leaders of Mexico.

_____   1. *His* birthplace was Oaxaca, Mexico.

_____   2. In 1847, *he* was elected governor of the Mexican state of Oaxaca.

_____ 3. At that time, the people of Mexico had few freedoms; Santa Anna ruled *them* with an iron hand.

_____ 4. Juárez and other local leaders opposed *him*.

_____ 5. *Their* dreams for greater freedom stalled when Santa Anna sent Juárez out of Mexico.

_____ 6. When Juárez returned to Mexico in 1855, *he* became minister of justice.

_____ 7. *Our* textbook states that one of Juárez's greatest deeds was putting through the Juárez Law.

_____ 8. *It* took away some powers from the army and the clergy and gave more rights to the citizens of Mexico.

_____ 9. Juárez was rewarded in 1861 when the people elected *him* president of Mexico.

_____ 10. Today, *we* credit Juárez for bringing religious freedom and civil rights to the people of Mexico.

EXERCISE 2   Writing a Poem with Personal Pronouns

On your own paper, write a poem of at least ten lines about how friendship can exist between people who are very different. In your poem, describe the differences between two friends. Use at least two examples of each of the three cases of pronouns. Underline each pronoun that you use.

EX. *I am wildfire.*

You are rain.

And yet we are friends.

MODULE 7: USING PRONOUNS CORRECTLY

NOMINATIVE CASE PRONOUNS

7a   The *subject of a verb* is always in the nominative case.

EXAMPLES   Do **they** enjoy country music? [*They* is the subject of *Do enjoy*.]

               He and **I** watched the show. [*He* and *I* are the two parts of the compound subject of *watched*.]

To choose the correct pronoun for use in a compound subject, try each form of the pronoun separately.

EXAMPLE   Oskar and (*me, I*) play in a band.

               Me play in a band. [incorrect use of objective case]

               I play in a band. [correct use of nominative case]

ANSWER   Oskar and **I** play in a band.

7b   A *predicate nominative* is always in the nominative case.

A *predicate nominative* is a noun or pronoun that follows a linking verb and explains or identifies the subject of the sentence. A pronoun used as a predicate nominative always follows a form of the verb *be* or a verb phrase ending in *be* or *been*.

EXAMPLES   The captain of the team is **I**. [*I* follows the linking verb *is* and identifies the subject, *captain*.]

               The owners of the store are Marsha and **he**. [*He* follows the verb *are* and identifies, along with *Marsha*, the subject, *owners*.]

EXERCISE 3   Identifying Nominative Case Pronouns

Complete each of the following sentences by underlining the correct pronoun or pronoun pair in parentheses.

    EX.   1.   Elsie and (*he, him*) are planning an Earth Day project.

1.   The contestants on the quiz show were (*him and me, he and I*).

2.   The person who called may have been (*she, her*).

3.   Naturally, (*she and I, her and me*) will help at the carwash.

4.   The most comfortable shoes are (*they, them*).

5.   Dr. Ramírez and (*us, we*) are meeting to plan the tournament.

6.   Amanda and (*I, me*) are working together on our research reports.

7.   The judges for the creative writing contest might be Ms. Robinson and (*them, they*).

8.   It was (*we, us*) who donated the set of encyclopedias for the library book sale.

9.   Have (*they, them*) visited South America before?

10.   Could it have been (*him, he*)?

11.   The big winners would be (*she, her*) and Ramona.

12.   Did (*I, me*) ever seem this happy before?

13.   (*They, Them*) always work together on their boat.

14.   (*We, Us*) sat down to think it over.

15.   Karen and (*I, me*) joined the soccer team on the same day.

EXERCISE 4   Proofreading Sentences for Correct Use of Nominative Case Pronouns

If a sentence below contains the wrong form of a pronoun, draw a line through the pronoun, and write the correct form above it. Some sentences are correct.

EX.   1.   Juan Carlos the First and ~~her~~ were the rulers of Spain.

she

1.   Our foreign exchange students this year are Kamaria and him.

2.   The team member who scored the most points was he.

3.   Him and I were both born in Laos.

4.   Two successful Cuban American singers are Gloria Estefan and her.

5.   Will he and me perform after Juanita?

6.   The winners of the award should have been her and I.

7.   Was it he who said, "Don't give up yet"?

8.   Perhaps you and me should volunteer for cleanup duty.

9.   That night, they announced that the winners were us!

10.   The drama coach said that he and me could apply for the two jobs as understudies.

PRONOUNS AS DIRECT OBJECTS

7c   The *direct object* of a verb is always in the objective case.

A *direct object* is a noun or pronoun that receives the action of a verb or that shows the result of the action.

EXAMPLES   The officer directed **me** to the right address. [*Me* tells *whom* the officer directed.]

Teresa gave **them** to her sister. [*Them* tells *what* Teresa gave.]

To choose the correct pronoun for use as a compound direct object, try each form of the pronoun separately.

EXAMPLE   The audience applauded Geraldo and (*I, me*).

The audience applauded *I*. [incorrect use of nominative case]

The audience applauded *me*. [correct use of objective case]

ANSWER   The audience applauded Geraldo and **me**.

EXERCISE 5   Choosing Correct Pronoun Forms

Complete each sentence below by writing an appropriate pronoun on the line or lines provided. Use a variety of pronouns, but do not use *you* or *it*. Make sure that each pronoun you choose makes sense in the sentence.

EX.   1. Fran took her brother and _____*me*_____ to a concert.

1. Someone called _____ extremely late last night.

2. Please help _____ with the assignment.

3. Did you see _____ at the library?

4. The child answered _____ politely.

5. Professional scouts contacted _____ and _____ after the game.

6. Simon and Rebecca told _____ about their visit to Israel.

7. Tomorrow night my brother will drive _____ to the mall.

8. Dr. Maldonado treated _____ and the other hikers for frostbite.

9. The orchestra leader thanked _____ and _____ for attending the concert.

10. Aunt Maribeth surprised _____ by coming to rehearsal.

EXERCISE 6   Proofreading for Correct Pronoun Case

Draw a line through each pronoun that is used incorrectly in the paragraph below. Write the correct pronoun in the space above the word. Some sentences are correct.

me
EX.   [1] They sent Zahara and ~~I~~ to the regional meeting.

[1] The members of our International Club surprised and pleased Zahara and I at the last meeting. [2] They chose she and me as representatives for the regional meeting. [3] They told me it was because Zahara is from East Africa and I am from Santiago, Chile. [4] Our international experiences have introduced we to many different cultures and beliefs. [5] Many students in our school, and particularly members of the International Club, have helped her and I in our new surroundings in the United States. [6] Now they are helping she and I in a whole new way. [7] They are sending us to the meeting to talk about how the city government might help students from foreign countries. [8] Zahara and I will tell you and they all about the meeting as soon as we return. [9] Or can you join she and I at the next meeting of the International Club? [10] Our meetings are on the first Tuesday of the month; I'm sure you'll enjoy they. [11] Zahara showed I some African artwork from her country. [12] I showed she a painting my father had done. [13] Zahara enjoys museums and often goes to visit they. [14] I enjoy them, too, but I like soccer games more. [15] All in all, everyone has treated we very well.

MODULE 7: USING PRONOUNS CORRECTLY

INDIRECT OBJECTS AND OBJECTS OF PREPOSITIONS

7d   The *indirect object* of a verb is always in the objective case.

An *indirect object* is a noun or pronoun that tells *to whom* or *for whom* something is done.

EXAMPLES   Hadiya sent **him** a birthday card. [*Him* tells *to whom* Hadiya sent a birthday card.]

Could you make **me** a sandwich? [*Me* tells *for whom* you could make a sandwich.]

To choose the correct pronoun for use in a compound indirect object, try each form of the pronoun separately in the sentence.

EXAMPLE   Emilio Estevez sent Melba and (*she, her*) an autographed photo. Emilio Estevez sent *she* an autographed photo. [incorrect use of nominative case] Emilio Estevez sent *her* an autographed photo. [correct use of objective case]

ANSWER   Emilio Estevez sent Melba and **her** an autographed photo.

EXERCISE 7   Using Pronouns as Indirect Objects

Complete each of the following sentences by writing an appropriate pronoun on the line or lines provided. Use a variety of pronouns, but do not use *you* or *it*.

EX.   1. Did Lorenzo loan his sister and _____*him*_____ money for the tickets?

1.   We gave _____ an award for being such a great coach.

2.   Will you loan _____ your copy of the script?

3.   When she returned to Somalia, Tabia sent _____ a note.

4.   The counselor gave Kareem and _____ some very good advice about scholarships.

5.   At lunch, Dolores told _____ and _____ a joke.

6.   When I did the job well, the boss offered _____ a better one.

7.   She mailed _____ all of our camping equipment.

8.   Mattie cooked _____ his favorite meal after the show.

9.   Ginette blushed when Alfredo handed _____ the flowers.

10.   It took six months for my cousin to write _____ a letter.

7e　　**The *object of a preposition* is always in the objective case.**

A *prepositional phrase* is a group of words consisting of a preposition, a noun or pronoun that serves as the object of the preposition, and any modifiers of that object.

EXAMPLES　　　for **me**　　　after Meredith and **him**　　in front of **us**

EXERCISE 8　　Choosing Correct Pronouns as Objects of Prepositions

Complete each sentence below by underlining the correct pronoun or pair of pronouns in parentheses.

EX. 1.　The musical was directed by (*he and she, him and her*).

1.　To my classmates and (*I, me*), Anzu and Ima Asato are very talented twin sisters.

2.　They wrote our class musical for (*we, us*).

3.　Thanks to (*them, they*), our musical won second place in the city music festival.

4.　Perhaps you read the article in the *Kansas City Star* about their family and (*they, them*).

5.　Because their father, a member of the Kansas City Symphony, helped them, we should send a thank-you note to (*he, him*).

6.　Between (*you and I, you and me*), the music was beautiful.

7.　Listen to (*I, me*) while I play the main theme on the piano.

8.　Jim and I were lucky that Ima was standing right in front of (*we, us*) in the chorus during the performance.

9.　We could listen to (*she, her*) as she sang, and we followed along.

10.　The entire cast got tapes of the music from (*they, them*) as gifts on opening night.

MODULE 7: USING PRONOUNS CORRECTLY

REVIEW EXERCISE

A.   Identifying Correct Pronoun Form

Complete each sentence below by underlining the correct pronoun in parentheses. On the line before the sentence, identify the pronoun's use in the sentence. Write *s.* for *subject*, *p.n.* for *predicate nominative*, *d.o.* for *direct object*, *i.o.* for *indirect object*, or *o.p.* for *object of a preposition*.

EX. __*p.n.*__   1.   That must be (*her*, <u>*she*</u>) at the door.

_____   1.   Please save two seats for Maisie and (*I*, *me*).

_____   2.   Our coach offered the younger students and (*they*, *them*) some pointers.

_____   3.   Many people thanked Ms. Tan and (*we*, *us*) for our posters in the cafeteria.

_____   4.   You never guessed that the person in the gorilla costume was (*I*, *me*)!

_____   5.   Whenever it rains hard, my sisters and (*I*, *me*) have to put towels around the door.

_____   6.   The Korean family that just moved into the neighborhood thanked (*we*, *us*) for the welcome basket.

_____   7.   Maria shared her grandmother's recipe for salsa with Jamyce and (*he*, *him*).

_____   8.   Somewhere along the way, Shani and (*she*, *her*) misplaced their house keys.

_____   9.   Show Ada May and (*I*, *me*) your drawing when you are finished.

_____   10. It may have been (*they*, *them*) who sent these flowers.

_____   11. Was it (*we*, *us*) who had the winning ticket?

_____   12. Ontario is a place that (*he*, *him*) has always wanted to visit.

_____   13. Thanks to (*they*, *them*), there are no more mosquitoes in the backyard.

_____   14. If you hurry, (*I*, *me*) will be able to meet you at the restaurant.

_____   15. The drama club honored Rita by giving (*she*, *her*) the prize for best play.

B. Proofreading for Correct Pronoun Forms

Draw a line through each pronoun that is used incorrectly in the paragraph below. Write the correct pronoun in the space above the word. Some sentences are correct.

me
EX.   [1] To Mavis and ~~I~~, Ronnie Milsap is the greatest country singer of all time.

[1] Country singer Ronnie Milsap, who is blind, has given we many memorable songs. [2] When Ronnie was six, his parents sent he to the Governor Morehead School for the Blind in Raleigh, North Carolina. [3] There, his classmates and him received excellent training in music. [4] Ronnie and them learned to play musical instruments, and he became especially interested in the piano and the violin. [5] After he left Morehead, he went to college in Georgia. [6] He entered the music business, and it is him that one can hear playing the piano on several of Elvis Presley's early hits. [7] By 1973, many people had heard about he because of his work on Presley's hit "Kentucky Rain" and many others. [8] In 1973, RCA offered him a contract to record his own songs. [9] My sister Mavis and me have collected all twenty-three of the albums he recorded with RCA. [10] The hit singles "Smoky Mountain Rain" and "Stranger in My House" are the favorites of both Mavis and I.

C. Writing a Friendly Note

On your own paper, write a note to a friend, telling about a movie you recently saw and enjoyed. Describe the major characters and the main events. In your letter, use five nominative and five objective case pronouns correctly. When you have finished writing, underline all of the pronouns. Above each pronoun, identify its use. Write *s.* for *subject,* *p.n.* for *predicate nominative,* *d.o.* for *direct object,* *i.o.* for *indirect object,* or *o.p.* for *object of a preposition.*

EX.   *Dear Marvin,*

     s.   *s.*   *o.p.*
     I just saw a great movie today. <u>*You*</u> *will enjoy all the action in* <u>*it.*</u>

MODULE 7: USING PRONOUNS CORRECTLY
WHO *AND* WHOM

7f   **Use *who* and *whoever* in the nominative case. Use *whom* and *whomever* in the objective case.**

NOTE   In spoken English, the use of *whom* is becoming less common. In fact, when speaking, you may correctly begin any question with *who*, regardless of the grammar of the sentence.

7g   **The use of *who* or *whom* in a subordinate clause depends on how the pronoun functions in the clause.**

When choosing whether to use *who* or *whom* in a subordinate clause, follow these steps.

Step 1:   Find the subordinate clause in the sentence.

Step 2:   Decide how the pronoun is used in the clause—as subject, predicate nominative, object of the verb, or object of a preposition.

Step 3:   Determine the case of the pronoun according to the rules of standard English.

Step 4:   Select the correct form of the pronoun.

EXAMPLE   I know (*who, whom*) wrote the note.

Step 1:   The clause is (*who, whom*) *wrote the note.*

Step 2:   In this clause, the pronoun is used as the subject of the verb *wrote.*

Step 3:   A pronoun used as a subject should be in the nominative case.

Step 4:   The nominative form is *who.*

ANSWER   I know **who** wrote the note.

NOTE   No words outside the clause affect the case of the pronoun. In the example above, the entire clause is used as a direct object of the verb *know*, but the pronoun *who* is used as a subject (nominative case) within the clause.

Frequently, *whom* in subordinate clauses is omitted (understood).

EXAMPLE   The man (*whom*) I voted for is Julian Washington.

EXERCISE 9   Classifying Pronouns Used in Subordinate Clauses and Identifying Correct Forms

Complete each sentence below by underlining the correct pronoun form in parentheses. On the line before the sentence, identify the pronoun's use in the clause. Write *s.* for *subject*, *p.n.* for *predicate nominative*, *d.o.* for *direct object*, or *o.p.* for *object of a preposition*.

EX. __*p.n.*__ 1. Do you know (*who*, *whom*) they are?

_____ 1. The student for (*who*, *whom*) I'm saving this seat should arrive shortly.

_____ 2. (*Whoever*, *Whomever*) you invite to the concert will be happy to go with you.

_____ 3. Did you talk to (*whoever*, *whomever*) you gave the plates for the party?

_____ 4. Mr. Ignacio is the Navajo artist (*who*, *whom*) we saw on television last night.

_____ 5. I haven't decided for (*who*, *whom*) I made this necklace.

_____ 6. Can you predict (*who*, *whom*) will win the class election?

_____ 7. Please tell me (*who*, *whom*) the owner of the store is.

_____ 8. The South American ruler (*who*, *whom*) we are now studying is Juan Perón.

_____ 9. (*Whoever*, *Whomever*) enters the contest must write a poem.

_____ 10. Tell us (*who*, *whom*) you saw at the bowling alley last night.

_____ 11. The sentry hailed (*whoever*, *whomever*) came up the path.

_____ 12. The judges will vote for (*whoever*, *whomever*) seems to be most worthy.

_____ 13. Can't you see (*who*, *whom*) really wants it more?

_____ 14. They named (*who*, *whom*) the winner is.

_____ 15. It's easy to see that (*whoever*, *whomever*) runs the fastest will arrive the soonest.

_____ 16. We thanked Deniz because he was (*who*, *whom*) brought the latkes.

_____ 17. Isabel gave the costumes to the actors to (*who*, *whom*) they were assigned.

_____ 18. Do you know Maribeth, (*who*, *whom*) I met yesterday?

_____ 19. How did Justin learn (*who*, *whom*) our new neighbor is?

_____ 20. Ken sent oranges to (*whoever*, *whomever*) he heard from first.

MODULE 7: USING PRONOUNS CORRECTLY

APPOSITIVES AND INCOMPLETE CONSTRUCTIONS

7h **Pronouns used with *appositives* are in the same case as the words to which they refer.**

An *appositive* is a noun or pronoun that follows another noun or pronoun to identify or explain it.

EXAMPLES   The judge announced the winners, Bart and **me**. [Since *winners* is the direct object of the verb *announced*, the pronoun *me*, in apposition with *winners*, must be in the objective case.]

We runners must train hard. [As subject of the sentence, *We* is in the nominative case. The noun *runners*, which identifies *We*, is the appositive.]

To choose the correct pronoun for use with an appositive or as an appositive, try the sentence with only the pronoun.

EXAMPLE   Two actors, Gina and (*me, I*), won awards on opening night. Gina and *me* won awards on opening night. [incorrect use of objective case]

Gina and *I* won awards on opening night. [correct use of nominative case]

ANSWER   Two actors, Gina and I, won awards on opening night.

EXERCISE 10   Identifying Correct Pronouns as Appositives

Complete each of the following sentences by underlining the correct pronoun form in parentheses.

EX.   1.   My cousins, Rachel and (<u>he</u>, *him*), are visiting from San Juan.

1.   The coach gave the fullbacks, Paulo and (*he, him*), a pep talk.

2.   The doctors thanked the nurses, Jobelle and (*I, me*).

3.   At the end of the concert, the musicians, (*we, us*), played four encores.

4.   Please offer more food to your guests, Charles and (*she, her*).

5.   The best athletes in the class, you and (*he, him*), might be called to the stage.

6.   Several people, the board and (*they, them*), elected a new president last year.

7.   The head cheerleaders, she and (*I, me*), ran the practice.

8.   The school newspaper paid a lot of attention to the basketball players, the forwards and (*we, us*).

9.   The last campers in the water, Manuel and (*I, me*), still reached the raft on time.

10.   The task of going for help was given to the best sailors on the lake, (*she, her*) and (*he, him*).

7i When *than* or *as* introduces an incomplete construction, use the form of the pronoun that would be correct if the construction were completed.

Notice how pronouns change the meaning of sentences with incomplete constructions.

EXAMPLES   I like Cleon better than **she**.
I like Cleon better than **her**.

In the first example, the nominative case pronoun *she* is the subject of an understood verb; *I like Cleon better than she [likes Cleon]*. In the second example, the objective case pronoun *her* is the object of an understood verb; *I like Cleon better than [I like] her*.

EXERCISE 11   Completing Incomplete Constructions and Classifying Pronoun Forms

Beginning with *than* or *as*, write the understood clause for each of the following sentences, on the line after it. Use the correct form of the pronoun. Then identify the pronoun in the completed clause by writing *s.* for *subject* or *obj.* for *object*. Some items may have more than one correct answer.

EX.   1.   Leroy is taller than (*I, me*). *than I am (s.)*

1. Can you swim to the end of the pool as fast as (*she, her*)?

   _____

2. You have called Mateo more often than (*I, me*).

   _____

3. I am just as good a writer as (*he, him*).

   _____

4. We have known Phoebe longer than (*they, them*).

   _____

5. Many people pay higher monthly rents than (*we, us*).

   _____

MODULE 7: USING PRONOUNS CORRECTLY

MODULE REVIEW

A. Correcting Pronoun Forms

Draw a line through each incorrect pronoun in the sentences below. On the line before each sentence, write the correct pronoun form.

EX. _____*I*_____ 1. Both of the applicants, Johan and me, took part-time jobs.

_____ 1. Katya speaks Spanish far better than her.

_____ 2. Mrs. Macavoy rented a canoe and prepared a picnic for Percy and I.

_____ 3. After the ballgame, the coach and me talked about my pitching.

_____ 4. Us residents of Benton Avenue have begun a neighborhood recycling campaign.

_____ 5. I can't believe that it was him who sent me this beautiful poem!

_____ 6. Do you know yet who you are inviting to the class dance?

_____ 7. The letter may have been written by one of my brothers, Juan or he.

_____ 8. I will give a reward to whomever finds my lost cat.

_____ 9. Have you decided to work for they?

_____ 10. The store owner gave both clerks, Mona and I, generous raises.

_____ 11. Someone should ask we students our opinion.

_____ 12. Wouldn't you like to go with she and me to the party?

_____ 13. To who do you think the principal was speaking?

_____ 14. We invited Helen and Frank to stay, but them wanted to get an early start.

_____ 15. Well, they did a good job, whomever it was.

_____ 16. Her and I have been friends since the first day of school.

_____ 17. Our history teacher told we honor students that we could do extra work.

_____ 18. Sometimes in the evenings my sister and him would sing folk songs together.

_____ 19. Mother wondered whom would speak first.

_____ 20. Us scuba divers like to explore coral reefs.

B. Proofreading a Paragraph for Correct Pronoun Forms

Draw a line through each pronoun that is used incorrectly in the paragraph below. Write the correct pronoun in the space above the word. Some sentences are correct.

who
EX. [1] The people ~~whom~~ see the baskets say that they are beautiful.

[1] When my family and me were in South Carolina last summer, we bought a beautiful sweet-grass basket. [2] The women whom make the baskets are African American. [3] Them and their relatives have woven and sewn these beautiful crafts for many years. [4] The people to who credit is given for bringing this art form to the United States were brought here as slaves from West Africa about three hundred years ago. [5] We had never seen sweet-grass baskets before, so we asked the women all about them. [6] Mrs. Washington told my sister and I that the other basket makers and her go to marshy fields to collect the sweet grass that grows wild there. [7] Then they bind together the coarse grass and stitch it into place. [8] The lady to who we spoke said that she takes at least ten hours to sew a basket. [9] Then she told my father and I about new problems that are facing the basket makers. [10] The fields of sweet grass are disappearing, and the art and the tradition of the basket makers might very well disappear with them.

C. Writing Interview Questions and Answers

As a feature writer for a sports magazine, you are to interview a celebrity sports figure. He or she might be a star in hockey, auto racing, basketball, or any other sport that you choose. On your own paper, write at least ten questions that you would ask about this person's background, accomplishments, and future goals. From magazines, newspapers, and biographies, gather information and details about this person. Use your research to write the answers that the person might give. Be sure to use the correct forms of personal pronouns in your questions and answers.

EX.   *Wayne Gretzky*
   1. *Among all the positions, why did you choose to be a goalie?*

COMPARISON OF MODIFIERS

Positive, comparative, and *superlative* are the three degrees of comparison for adjectives and adverbs.

POSITIVE	Robert told a **funny** joke.
COMPARATIVE	Kim told a joke that was **funnier** than Robert's was.
SUPERLATIVE	Of all of them, Charlie told the **funniest** joke.

8a **A one-syllable modifier regularly forms its comparative and superlative degrees by adding** *–er* **and** *–est.*

POSITIVE	My cat is **wet** from the rain.
COMPARATIVE	My dog is **wetter** than my cat is.
SUPERLATIVE	My horse is the **wettest** of my three pets.

8b **Some two-syllable modifiers form their comparative and superlative degrees by adding** *–er* **and** *–est.* **Others form these degrees by using** *more* **and** *most* **or** *less* **and** *least.*

Positive	Comparative	Superlative
windy	windier	windiest
careful	more careful	most careful
anxious	less anxious	least anxious

NOTE   Some two-syllable modifiers, such as *common,* may use either *–er* and *–est* or *more/less* and *most/least.*

8c **Modifiers that have more than two syllables form their comparative and superlative degrees with** *more/less* **and** *most/least.*

Positive	Comparative	Superlative
original	more original	most original
beautiful	less beautiful	least beautiful

8d **Some modifiers use irregular methods of forming their comparative and superlative degrees.**

Do not add *–er* and *–est* or *more/less* and *most/least* to irregularly formed comparisons.

Positive	Comparative	Superlative
good	better	best
bad	worse	worst
many/much	more	most

EXERCISE 1   Forming Degrees of Comparison with Modifiers

On the lines below, write the comparative and superlative degrees of each of the following modifiers. Use a dictionary as necessary.

EX. 1. large   *larger*   *largest*

1. exciting   _____   _____

2. happy   _____   _____

3. delightful   _____   _____

4. little   _____   _____

5. quickly   _____   _____

6. blue   _____   _____

7. afraid   _____   _____

8. suspicious   _____   _____

9. round   _____   _____

10. far   _____   _____

EXERCISE 2   Proofreading for Correct Comparative and Superlative Forms

Underline the comparative or superlative form of the modifier in each sentence below. If the form is incorrect, write the correct form above it.

more careful

EX. 1. Avis will be <u>carefuller</u> than your last mechanic.

1.   Pelé was certainly one of the successfullest soccer players in the world.

2.   The judges thought that Alice's poem was originaller than mine.

3.   This hurricane was the destructivest that we've had in years!

4.   That man looks like the most happy worker in the city.

5.   Of all the foods here, sushi is the least likely to contain fat.

6.   Which do you like better, traveling by train or by airplane?

7.   I'm not sure which of those two is the more safe way to travel.

8.   Of all the cities we visited in Japan, Kyoto is the beautifullest.

9.   I saw several silk kimonos on sale, but I decided to buy the least expensive one.

10. This trip was even gooder than the one we took last year.

USES OF COMPARATIVE AND SUPERLATIVE FORMS

8e **Use the comparative degree when comparing two things. Use the superlative degree when comparing more than two.**

COMPARATIVE   The little red pepper is **spicier** than the green one.

SUPERLATIVE   This little red pepper is the **spiciest** one of all.

NOTE   In everyday conversation, people sometimes use the superlative degree when comparing two things: *I pitch best with my right hand.*

8f **Include the word *other* or *else* when comparing one thing with others that belong in the same group.**

NONSTANDARD   Anaba writes better than any student in her class.

STANDARD   Anaba writes better than any **other** student in her class.

NONSTANDARD   Uncle Luis is funnier than anyone in my family.

STANDARD   Uncle Luis is funnier than anyone **else** in my family.

8g **Avoid double comparisons.**

A *double comparison* is incorrect because it contains both *–er* and *more/less* or *–est* and *most/least.*

NONSTANDARD   I think Tom Landry is more older than your father.

STANDARD   I think Tom Landry is **older** than your father.

8h **Be sure your comparisons are clear.**

UNCLEAR   The restaurants in Rockport are cheaper than New York City.

CLEAR   The restaurants in Rockport are cheaper than the restaurants in New York City.

EXERCISE 3   Identifying and Correcting Modifiers

For each of the following sentences, underline the error in the use of modifiers. Rewrite each sentence correctly on the line provided.

EX.   1. This film is <u>best than the one</u> we saw last week.

        This film is better than the one we saw last week.

1. Indian films are often more longer than American films.

    _____

2. Bombay must contain the greater number of film posters in the world.

    _____

3. Tien liked this film more than anyone who saw it.

_____

4. This comedy is the least funniest in this film festival.

_____

5. The films of Mr. Satyajit Ray are more seriouser than those of Mr. B. Kapoor.

_____

6. Of my two sisters, Nora knows most about film directors.

_____

7. This theater is much less comfortable than yesterday.

_____

8. The movie's made by students are not as polished as experienced directors.

_____

9. It is certainly more hotter outside than it is in the theater.

_____

10. Directors in India make more films than directors in any country in the world.

_____

11. In India, the price of a movie ticket is cheapest than in the United States.

_____

12. The length of the movie is least important than the entertainment it provides.

_____

13. Kapoor wants to get the most best stars and the most best music for his movies.

_____

14. Will Kapoor continue to be India's bigger filmmaker?

_____

15. One of his movies was the larger production ever made in India.

_____

MODULE 8: USING MODIFIERS CORRECTLY
DANGLING MODIFIERS

8i **A modifying phrase or clause that does not clearly and sensibly modify a word or group of words in a sentence is called a *dangling modifier*.**

When a modifying phrase containing a verbal comes at the beginning of a sentence, the phrase is followed by a comma. Immediately after that comma should come the word that the phrase modifies.

UNCLEAR   Visiting Philadelphia, several museums interested me.

  CLEAR   Visiting Philadelphia, I was interested in several museums.

UNCLEAR   To see Henry Ossawa Tanner's work, a visit to the Philadelphia Museum of Art is necessary.

  CLEAR   To see Henry Ossawa Tanner's work, you must visit the Philadelphia Museum of Art.

To correct a dangling modifier, rearrange the words in the sentence, and add or change words to make the meaning logical and clear.

 DANGLING   Arriving on a holiday, the museum was closed.

 CORRECTED   Arriving on a holiday, we found the museum closed.

NOTE   A sentence may appear to have a dangling modifier when *you* is the understood subject. In such cases, the modifier is not dangling; it is modifying the understood subject.

       EXAMPLE   To paint well, (you) spend a lot of time drawing.

EXERCISE 4   Revising Sentences by Eliminating Dangling Modifiers

On the line after each of the following sentences, indicate how you would revise the sentence to eliminate the dangling modifier. As shown by the example, you need not write the whole sentence.

  EX.   1. Looking at one drawing, the signature surprised me.
           *drawing, I was surprised by the signature.*_____

  1. Displayed in one gallery, we enjoyed the Japanese woodcuts._____

      _____

  2. To see everything on this floor, a plan is necessary._____

      _____

3. Looking at the watercolors, some looked like oil paintings._____

_____

4. Hung on several walls, Sharon read placards telling about the artist's life.

_____

5. To prevent damage, many pieces were covered with plastic shields by the officials.

_____

6. There will be a special show next month of local photography.

_____

7. Some winter scenes gave us chills painted in grays and whites.

_____

8. My favorite colors were used in several paintings, which are mainly reds and yellows.

_____

9. Along the New England coast, one group of photographs showed storm scenes.

_____

10. Expecting a large crowd, arrangements were made by the museum to change the viewing hours.

_____

EXERCISE 5   Writing Sentences with Introductory Modifiers

Write ten complete sentences using the introductory modifiers below. Be sure the word that the phrase modifies immediately follows the comma. Write your sentences on your own paper.

EX.   1. Wearing bug repellent,
      Wearing bug repellent, we ventured into the woods.

1. Waving a camera,

2. To create memorable pictures,

3. Working quickly,

4. Covered with mosquito bites,

5. To photograph hummingbirds,

6. After listening to the report,

7. Walking to school,

8. Made from leather,

9. Creeping around the door,

10. To talk on this pay telephone,

MISPLACED MODIFIERS

8j   A *misplaced modifier* is a phrase or clause that sounds awkward because it modifies the wrong word or group of words.

Modifying phrases should be placed as near as possible to the word or words they modify.

MISPLACED   The picture was taken at the August Moon Festival of the little girl in a yellow costume.

CORRECTED   The picture **of the little girl in a yellow costume** was taken at the August Moon Festival.

Adjective clauses and adverb clauses should be placed so that they are clearly linked to the words they modify.

MISPLACED   Before you leave, get the atlas from the table that you need.

CORRECTED   Before you leave, get the atlas **that you need** from the table.

EXERCISE 6   Revising Sentences by Correcting Misplaced Modifiers

Underline the misplaced modifier in each of the following sentences. Indicate where the modifier should appear in the sentence by inserting a caret (∧).

EX.   1.   The detective ∧ questioned Ms. O'Rourke <u>with the dark beard</u>.

1.   Written by Henry David Thoreau, I admire the simple country life portrayed in *Walden*.

2.   We could hear the tornado approaching from our basement shelter.

3.   Leonora went to her room after her brother had left for the video arcade to do some homework.

4.   The car will win an award that is the most fuel-efficient.

5.   We read about the candidates who are running for mayor in the Sunday paper.

6.   In the sky last night, our astronomy class enjoyed watching a meteor shower.

7.   Their dog was waiting at the door looking very excited and wagging its tail.

8.   We drove Mr. Mason from his house to the mall, who needed to run an errand.

9. Always a very caring person, Rebecca decided to become a nurse at the age of twelve.

10. The neighbor's dogs frightened the Yamaguchis' new baby barking at night.

11. The salad is in the refrigerator for your lunch.

12. I willingly admit that I might have given up and gone home in her situation.

13. Mrs. Worthington gave some of her prize-winning roses to her neighbor arranged in a white basket.

14. The rusty, green van belongs to our next-door neighbor that is parked in the driveway.

15. Nikki drove the family car wearing sunglasses and a leather cap.

16. The Allentown Community Choir rehearsed a new song paying careful attention to the rhythm.

17. Cheering the loudest, the prize was awarded to the team.

18. During the fire drill, the students were asked to leave the room quietly by the teacher.

19. The puppy sat in the doorway scratching its head.

20. Phoebe got all the supplies from the store that she needed.

21. Granny told me a story about getting caught in a storm sitting in her chair near the window.

22. They fixed the bike's flat quickly working together.

23. I work for my money hard.

24. You can find the photographs that Dad took of your great-grandparents in one of these old photo albums.

25. The old family home sat on a hill needing repair.

MODULE 8: USING MODIFIERS CORRECTLY

MODULE REVIEW

A. Revising Sentences by Correcting Modifiers

In the sentences below, correct all errors in the use of modifiers. Rewrite each sentence on your own paper.

EX. 1. Yo-Yo Ma must be one of the famousest cellists in the world.

1. *Yo-Yo Ma must be one of the most famous cellists in the world.*

1. These seats are more better than the ones we had last month.

2. In his seat I told my young cousin to sit quietly.

3. That pianist is better than any musician I've heard.

4. Sitting in the center of the hall, the music surrounded us.

5. The trio is playing the piece that you liked onstage now.

6. There are many families in the audience with children.

7. Later, a chorus will sing the familiarest songs from *The Wizard of Oz*.

8. Having seen the movie, the songs were enjoyed by the children.

9. Which song is your more favorite?

10. Moving her arms gracefully, we watched the conductor.

B. Using Modifiers Correctly in a Paragraph

In the following paragraph, underline any misplaced or incorrect modifiers. For misplaced modifiers, indicate where the modifier should appear in the sentence by inserting a caret (∧). For all other errors, write the corrections above the sentence.

EX. [1] Many people ∧ visit Nashville <u>who like music</u>.

[1] Of all the U. S. cities, Nashville is probably the one that is more famous for

country music. [2] However, people can enjoy a great variety of music who go there.

[3] In 1980, my parents enjoyed a performance of the Royal Laotian Classical Dance

Troupe, whose vacation included a visit to Nashville. [4] Before performing, fancy costumes and masks were put on. [5] Then the dancers told traditional stories using their costumes and their bodies. [6] The stories about ancient Laos that they told were more than six hundred years old. [7] The music is played on stringed and percussion instruments that accompanies the dances. [8] Originally performed only for the king of Laos and his court, the Nashville audience seemed to appreciate the royal dances.

[9] These dances for centuries have been passed from one generation to the next.

[10] Having heard so much about these dances, it should be interesting for me see them myself.

C.   Using Modifiers in an Adventure Story

As an author of adventure stories, you have jotted down the following list of phrases and clauses as prewriting for a new tale. On your own paper, use ten of the following phrases and clauses correctly to write your opening paragraph. To make sure that your paragraph does not have any dangling or misplaced modifiers, underline the modifiers you use, and draw arrows to the words they modify.

speeding down the mountainside	rubbing my bruised leg
while enjoying a brief rest	which I discovered by accident
to avoid falling in the canyon	from my experience as a rider
chased by a wild beast	to avoid being seen
that seemed safer	hearing a moaning sound
diving into the water	that caused my hair to curl
jumping off the speeding freight train	to escape the extreme engine heat
that was hidden inside a cave	creeping silently along
to save myself from certain disaster	hoping for some daylight
which later saved my life	that was under a rotted log

EX. that seemed safer

   My eyes darted around frantically as I searched for a path that seemed safer.

MODULE 9: A GLOSSARY OF USAGE
A, AN – BESIDE, BESIDES

This module presents an alphabetical list of common problems in English usage. Throughout the module, examples are labeled *standard* or *nonstandard*. **Standard English** is the most widely accepted form of English. **Nonstandard English** is language that does not follow the rules and guidelines of standard English.

a, an These ***indefinite articles*** refer to one of a general group.

EXAMPLES   Jaime ate **a** banana and **an** orange.

Crystal bought **an** umbrella and **a** uniform for work.

Use *a* before words beginning with a consonant sound; use *an* before words beginning with a vowel sound. In the example above, *a* is used before *uniform* because the *u* in *uniform* has a consonant sound.

affect, effect   *Affect* is a verb meaning "to influence." *Effect* used as a verb means "to accomplish." Used as a noun, *effect* means "the result of some action."

EXAMPLES   Did the happy story **affect** your mood?

The coach gave a speech to **effect** a change in the team's morale.

The sad story had a negative **effect** on me.

all the farther, all the faster   These phrases are used in some parts of the United States to mean "as far as" or "as fast as."

NONSTANDARD   One mile is all the farther he can run.

STANDARD   One mile is **as far as** he can run.

among See **between, among.**

and etc.   *Etc.* is an abbreviation of the Latin phrase *et cetera*, meaning "and other things." Thus, *and etc.* means "and and other things." Do not use *and* with *etc.*

EXAMPLE   During baseball practice, Philip worked on batting, fielding, throwing, ***etc.*** [not *and etc.*]

anywheres, everywheres, nowheres, somewheres Use these words without the final *s*.

EXAMPLE   I looked **everywhere** for that recipe. [not *everywheres*]

as See **like, as.**

at Do not use *at* after *where*.

NONSTANDARD   I don't know where she's at.

STANDARD   I don't know **where** she is.

> **beside, besides** *Beside* is a preposition that means "by the side of" someone or something. *Besides* as a preposition means "in addition to." As an adverb, *besides* means "moreover."
>
> EXAMPLES   Lily sat **beside** Natalya on the bus. [preposition]
> **Besides** cleaning his room, he has to wash the dishes. [preposition]
> I don't have enough money for the movie. **Besides,** I haven't finished my homework. [adverb]

EXERCISE 1   Solving Common Usage Problems

For each sentence below, underline the correct word or expression in parentheses.

EX.   1.   I like to use (*a, an*) straw.

1.   "This is (*all the farther, as far as*) I can swim," he panted as he climbed into the boat.

2.   (*Beside, Besides*) Shanaz, no one did well on the test.

3.   The pollution from that factory (*affects, effects*) the air quality of the entire region.

4.   Shiloh's puppy follows him (*everywheres, everywhere*).

5.   Sometimes I don't know where your head (*is, is at*)!

EXERCISE 2   Proofreading Sentences for Correct Usage

In each sentence below, draw a line through the error in usage, and write the correct form above it.

                                           somewhere
EX.   1.   The trunk with Grandma's heirlooms is ~~somewheres~~ in the attic.

1.   I hope Nicholas sits besides me at the play.

2.   The missing key was nowheres to be found.

3.   Does Rodrigo really practice the trombone for a hour each morning?

4.   No one seems to know where our next basketball game is at.

5.   Max has to dust the living room, set the table, arrange the flowers, and etc., before the guests arrive.

BETWEEN, AMONG – FEWER, LESS

---

between, among   Use *between* when you are referring to two things at a time, even though they may be part of a group consisting of more than two. Use *among* when you are thinking of a group rather than of separate things.

EXAMPLES   Place that plant **between** the piano and the chair.
Greetings were exchanged **between** the six guests. [Although there were more than two guests, the guests greeted one another in pairs, or two at a time.]
There was excitement **among** the fans when Irisa scored a goal. [The fans are thought of as a group in this situation.]

could of   Do not write *of* with the helping verb *could*. Write *could have*. Also avoid *ought to of, had of, should of, would of, might of,* and *must of*.

EXAMPLES   Jamila **could have** helped you. [not *could of*]
I **ought to have** made souvlakia for dinner. [not *ought to of*]

discover, invent   *Discover* means "to be the first to find, see, or learn about something that already exists." *Invent* means "to be the first to do or make something."

EXAMPLES   Edmond Halley **discovered** the comet that bears his name.
The piano was **invented** by Bartolomeo Cristofori in 1709.

effect, affect   See **affect, effect.**

everywheres   See **anywheres,** etc.

fewer, less   *Fewer* is used with plural words. *Less* is used with singular words. *Fewer* tells "how many"; *less* tells "how much."

EXAMPLES   **Fewer** people attended the festival this year.
The festival took up **less** space this year.

EXERCISE 3   Identifying Correct Usage

For each of the following sentences, underline the correct word or expression in parentheses.

EX.   1.   My ancestors lived (*somewheres, <u>somewhere</u>*) in El Salvador.

1.   We (*should have, should of*) left earlier.

2.   Thomas Edison (*discovered, invented*) the electric light.

3.   Did that hurricane (*affect, effect*) your town?

4.   I (*might have, might of*) taken that phone message.

5.   Mika sat on the lawn (*among, between*) the dandelions.

6.   The heat had a negative (*affect, effect*) on my energy level.

7.   When we checked the returns, we were surprised that (*fewer, less*) people donated money this month than last month.

8.   Lan (*must have, must of*) rehearsed for hours.

9.   I searched (*everywhere, everywheres*) for books about Indira Gandhi, a former prime minister of India.

10.   Jonas Salk (*discovered, invented*) a cure for polio.

11.   There was (*fewer, less*) room in the car than we had expected.

12.   Samuel and Liona (*ought to have, ought to of*) studied harder for their grammar quiz.

13.   My grandfather lives in Laos, a country (*among, between*) Vietnam and Thailand.

14.   Marco needs to (*affect, effect*) a detailed plan for our project.

15.   I had (*less, fewer*) homework assignments than usual, so I (*could have, could of*) helped you.

16.   I (*could have, could of*) won the race if only I hadn't gotten a cramp.

17.   The television program showed that the four thieves split the stolen money (*among, between*) themselves.

18.   Nathaniel has been having (*fewer, less*) headaches since he improved his diet.

19.   Working in their father's shop, the boys (*discovered, invented*) a burglar alarm.

20.   Thaddeus (*ought to have, ought to of*) signed up for that class when there was an opening.

had of See **could of.**

had ought, hadn't ought Unlike other verbs, *ought* is not used with *had*.

NONSTANDARD Jake had ought to budget his money; he hadn't ought to spend so much that he can't save any money.

STANDARD Jake **ought** to budget his money; he **ought not** to spend so much that he can't save any money.

invent, discover See **discover, invent.**

kind, sort, type The words *this, that, these,* and *those* should always agree in number with the words *kind, sort,* and *type.*

EXAMPLE Is **this type** of music more relaxing than **those** other **types?**

learn, teach *Learn* means "to acquire knowledge." *Teach* means "to instruct" or "to show how."

EXAMPLE I want to **learn** to speak Italian; do you think you can **teach** me?

leave, let *Leave* means "to go away" or "to depart from." *Let* means "to allow" or "to permit."

NONSTANDARD Leave Jamal go home.

STANDARD **Let** Jamal go home.

less See **fewer, less.**

like, as In informal English, the preposition *like* is often used as a conjunction meaning "as." In formal English, use *like* to introduce a prepositional phrase, and use *as* to introduce a subordinate clause.

EXAMPLES That building looks **like** a castle.
Please do the project **as** our teacher described.

might of, must of See **could of.**

nowheres See **anywheres,** etc.

of Do not use *of* with prepositions such as *inside, off,* or *outside.*

EXAMPLES I went **inside** the pantry. [not *inside of*]
I took some crackers **off** the top shelf. [not *off of*]
I walked **outside** the building. [not *outside of*]

ought to of See **could of.**

EXERCISE 4   Identifying Correct Usage

In each sentence below, underline the correct word or expression in parentheses.

EX.   1. Leon (*had ought, <u>ought</u>*) to attend the spring festival.

1. Ms. Gabriel will (learn, teach) the class about Martin Luther King, Jr.

2. Please (let, leave) my puppy play in the yard.

3. Did you find evidence that this (type, types) of moccasin was worn by many Native Americans?

4. Wyatt looks (as, like) his older sister.

5. We walked around (inside, inside of) the White House when we were in Washington, D.C.

EXERCISE 5   Correcting Errors in Usage

In the sentences below, draw a line through each error, and write the correct form above it. Some sentences contain more than one error.

EX.   1. Martina climbed ~~off of~~ her bicycle.   *off*

1. I would like to play my cello like Anthony does.

2. These kind of books learned us all about several kinds of inventions in ancient China.

3. That cave looked as a good camping spot, so we walked inside of it and looked around.

4. This kinds of enchilada is spicier than those kind.

5. We hadn't ought to swim without a lifeguard, even though the camp counselors learned us how to swim.

6. Please leave me go with you to the Cinco de Mayo parade.

7. The sea lion has whiskers like a cat does.

8. Those type of rugs are made in Afghanistan.

9. The ball flew over the outfield wall and landed outside of the park.

10. We had ought to wear our rain gear for the hike to the summit.

should of See **could of.**

some, somewhat In writing, do not use *some* for *somewhat* as an adverb.

NONSTANDARD   I enjoyed hiking in the woods some.

    STANDARD   I enjoyed hiking in the woods **somewhat.**

somewheres See **anywheres.**

sort See **kind**, etc.

teach See **learn, teach.**

than, then *Than* is a conjunction; *then* is an adverb.

EXAMPLES   That lamp is brighter **than** this one.
               I will stop at the market; **then** I will visit you.

them *Them* should not be used as an adjective. Use *those* or *these*.

EXAMPLE   Milagro enjoyed **those** long walks on the beach. [not *them*]

this here, that there The words *here* and *there* are unnecessary after *this* and *that*.

EXAMPLE   I like **this** wallpaper. [not *this here*]
               Ida likes **that** style. [not *that there*]

type See **kind**, etc.

when, where Do not use *when* or *where* incorrectly in writing a definition. Do not use *where* for *that*.

NONSTANDARD   A bialy is when you make a flat breakfast roll.

    STANDARD   A bialy is a flat breakfast roll.

    STANDARD   I heard in class **that** school is being canceled. [not *where*]

which, that, who The relative pronoun *who* refers to people only; *which* refers to things only; *that* refers to either people or things.

EXAMPLES   Annmarie is the one **who** ordered that sandwich. [person]
               That afghan, **which** is in the closet, was a birthday gift. [thing]
               Eli was the person **that** I wanted to meet. [person]
               The salsa **that** I made is in the refrigerator. [thing]

would of See **could of.**

EXERCISE 6   Correcting Errors in Usage

For each sentence below, underline the correct word or expression in parentheses.

EX.   1. (*Them*, *Those*) books are about tropical rain forests.

1. Shina is (*some*, *somewhat*) interested in (*this*, *this here*) topic.

2. Rain forests, (*which*, *who*) have rain almost every day, have no frost.

3. Hundreds of kinds of trees grow in (*these*, *them*) forests.

4. Shina told me (*where*, *that*) the canopy is the tops of the trees, and animals living there climb a long (*way*, *ways*) in search of food.

5. Southeast Asia's rain forest is taller (*than*, *then*) most.

EXERCISE 7   Correcting Errors in Usage

In the sentences below, draw a line through each error, and write the correct form above it. Some sentences contain more than one error.

EX.   1. I am ~~some~~ *somewhat* familiar with the Red Cross.

1. A short ways down the street, people were donating blood.

2. This here blood drive was being run by the Red Cross.

3. Them Red Cross volunteers help people all over the world.

4. Volunteers are when people give their time and services without having to and often without being paid.

5. Red Cross volunteers, which can be found in many countries, are paid with grateful smiles from them people they help.

6. The Red Crescent, who operates in Muslim countries, is part of the same group.

7. When there's a natural disaster, they might have to carry blood and medical supplies a long ways.

8. Often, their work is some dangerous.

9. Red Cross and Red Crescent volunteers often can help better then governments can.

10. My friend Mr. Azakian learned me about these volunteers.

MODULE 9: A GLOSSARY OF USAGE
DOUBLE NEGATIVES

In a *double negative*, two negative words are used when one is sufficient. Avoid double negatives in both writing and speaking.

hardly, scarcely The words *hardly* and *scarcely* both convey a negative meaning. Never use one of these words with another negative word.

EXAMPLES I **can hardly** believe that my sister is graduating. [not *can't*]
The park **has scarcely** enough swings. [not *hasn't*]

no, nothing, none Do not use one of these words with another negative word.

NONSTANDARD	We don't have no library books.
STANDARD	We **don't have any** library books.
STANDARD	We **have no** library books.
NONSTANDARD	I don't want nothing to do with the problem.
STANDARD	I **don't want anything** to do with the problem.
STANDARD	I **want nothing** to do with the problem.
NONSTANDARD	Kareena wanted tickets, but there weren't none left.
STANDARD	Kareena wanted tickets, but there **weren't any** left.
STANDARD	Kareena wanted tickets, but there **were none** left.

EXERCISE 8   Correcting Errors in Usage

Each of the sentences below contains at least one error in usage. Draw a line through each error, and write the correct form above it.

can hardly
EX.   1. Hector ~~can't hardly~~ believe he made the team.

1. I didn't have no plans last night, so I went for a long walk.

2. Kali's family owns a wonderful restaurant that hasn't scarcely ever had a slow moment.

3. Ricardo didn't buy nothing at the fruit and vegetable market.

4. Asa and I don't have no time to practice today, and we didn't hardly have any time yesterday.

5. We wanted to build a real wigwam, but there weren't no poles for the frame.

EXERCISE 9   Proofreading Paragraphs for Double Negatives

In the paragraph below, draw a line through the errors in usage. Write the correct form above the underlined error. Some sentences contain no errors.

can't (or can hardly)
EX.   [1] I ~~can't hardly~~ believe that I have never heard of this poet.

[1] Born in 1917 in Topeka, Kansas, Gwendolyn Brooks didn't hardly live there for

long. [2] She wasn't no adult, but just a teenager, when her poetry was first published in

the *Chicago Defender* and *American Childhood*. [3] At college, and later at the South

Side Community Art Center, Gwendolyn didn't miss no chance to improve her writing.

[4] As a result, she didn't hardly surprise people by winning several local poetry

contests. [5] Her poetry hadn't scarcely appeared in *Poetry* magazine before she

published her first book of poems, *A Street in Bronzeville*, in 1945. [6] The critics didn't

have nothing but praise for her work, and she received two awards in a row. [7] Winning

the awards meant that she wouldn't have to do nothing but write poetry for a while.

[8] In 1949, Ms. Brooks published *Annie Allen*, which didn't include none of her

previous work. [9] For these new poems, she won nothing no less important than the

1950 Pulitzer Prize in poetry. [10] No other black woman had never won this before.

[11] Ms. Brooks's style became more casual through the 1950s and 1960s, but the

change did not take away nothing from her humor and skill. [12] In the 1970s, the

themes of her writing were not different from the social issues of the times. [13] Her

children's stories and novels of the 1970s and 1980s didn't reflect these themes no less

than her poetry had. [14] At various times over the years, she went back to college—

not as a student, but as a teacher of poetry. [15] Perhaps nothing couldn't match the

honor given to Ms. Brooks in 1968 when she became the poet laureate of Illinois.

MODULE 9: A GLOSSARY OF USAGE
MODULE REVIEW

A. Identifying Errors in Usage

For each sentence below, underline the correct word or expression in parentheses.

EX. 1. The discussion (*between*, <u>*among*</u>) my classmates was about trains.

1. Did you read (*where*, *that*) railroads have been used since the 1500s?

2. These early (*types*, *type*) of rails were made of wood.

3. Trains were wagons that had to be pulled (*everywheres*, *everywhere*) by horses.

4. Steam railroads were (*discovered*, *invented*) in the 1800s.

5. Steam engines looked much (*like*, *as*) the diesel engines of today.

6. George Stephenson had a big (*effect*, *affect*) on this (*kinds*, *kind*) of transportation.

7. (*This here*, *This*) man built trains so that people could ride (*inside*, *inside of*) the cars.

8. Our teacher (*learned*, *taught*) us about the transcontinental railroad.

9. This (*must have*, *must of*) been one of the most important projects in U.S. history.

10. The construction of a nationwide railroad system immensely (*effected*, *affected*) the country's growth.

11. One thing that (*hadn't ought*, *ought not*) to be ignored is that immigrants (*which*, *who*) were mostly from China built this railroad.

12. Before the transcontinental railroad, there were (*fewer*, *less*) people in the West.

13. After the railroad was built, the United States went a long (*way*, *ways*) in growing as a nation.

14. The transcontinental railroad, (*beside*, *besides*) transporting people, enabled industries to expand to new areas.

15. For my project on the railroad, I am building (*a*, *an*) steam engine out of folded paper.

B. Using Words Correctly in Sentences

Because your friends respect your opinion, they often ask your advice on how to handle their problems. On your own paper, use fifteen of the words or expressions in this module to write sentences suggesting solutions to a few of your friends' problems. Underline the words or expressions you use.

EX. 1. _Learn_ the rules for using diving equipment before you try diving.

C. Writing a Letter

You are a diver on an expedition. Exploring the sea one morning, you come across a large sunken ship. You and your partner decide to enter it and look around. Later, when you are back on your ship, you decide to sit down and write a letter to a friend, describing your day and all that you saw in the sunken ship. In your letter, use five of the words or expressions covered in this module. Underline the words and the expressions that you use.

EX. Dear Lucia,

You _would have_ been interested in our discovery today.

MODULE 10: CAPITAL LETTERS

SENTENCES, PRONOUN I, *AND INTERJECTION* O

10a   Capitalize the first word in every sentence.

EXAMPLES   **The** bus is late.
We may be late for the game.

Traditionally, the first word of a line of poetry is capitalized.

EXAMPLE   **We** wandered freely in the park
Until the summer sky grew dark.

NOTE   Some writers do not always follow these capitalization rules. If you are quoting, use letters exactly as the author uses them in the source of the quotation.

10b   Capitalize the pronoun *I* **and the interjection** *O.*

Although it is rarely used, *O* is always capitalized. Generally, it is reserved for invocations and is followed by the name of the person or thing being addressed. You will more often use the interjection *oh*, which is not capitalized unless it is the first word of the sentence.

EXAMPLES   When **I** wake up my brother, **I** sometimes say, "**O** Sleepyhead, you will miss your bus."

We paddled safely through, but **oh,** what a struggle we had!

EXERCISE 1   Capitalizing Sentences in a Paragraph

In the following paragraph, underline the words that should begin with a capital letter.

EX.   <u>my</u> favorite section of the orchestra is the percussion section

1   drums, castanets, and xylophones are all percussion

2   instruments. the player strikes these instruments in some way to

3   make a sound. for striking, the player may use sticks, mallets, or

4   sometimes brushes. pitch, though, is not adjustable on some

5   percussion instruments. for a xylophone, the length of the bars

6   determines the pitch when you play it, but many drums are tuned

7   by a player. have you ever watched the timpanist tune a

8   kettledrum? the player adjusts the skin of the drum to make the

9   pitch higher or lower. in order to do this, the player uses a special

10   key to loosen or tighten the tuning pegs. i love to hear the

11   timpani in *Thus Spoke Zarathustra*. next year I hope to learn to

12   play the timpani in our school orchestra.

EXERCISE 2   Correcting Capitalization Errors in Sentences

In the sentences below, underline the words that have errors in capitalization.

EX. 1. If <u>i</u> could have three wishes, one would be "Give me three more wishes, <u>o</u> genie!"

1.   Do some holy books often address their readers, "o faithful believers"?

2.   the first snowfall is beautiful, but Oh, how i wish it were spring!

3.   We laughed when he said the punch line, "So i bit him."

4.   have you ever heard anyone say, "Woe is me!"?

5.   The team chanted, "o you Tigers! go! go! go!"

6.   are you buying cookies this year from the Girl Scouts?

7.   we studied the works of the Danish poet Johannes Ewald.

8.   Felipe Calderón was, i believe, president of Mexico from 2006–12.

9.   the Chinese poet Li Po lived from A.D. 701–762.

10. have you ever heard of the first-century Greek critic Longinus?

MODULE 10: CAPITAL LETTERS

PROPER NOUNS AND ADJECTIVES

10c   Capitalize proper nouns and proper adjectives.

A ***common noun*** names one of a group of people, places, or things. A ***proper noun*** names a particular person, place, or thing. ***Proper adjectives*** are formed from proper nouns.

Common nouns are not capitalized unless they begin a sentence or a direct quotation, or are included in a title. Proper nouns are always capitalized.

Common Nouns	Proper Nouns	Proper Adjectives
a country	Mexico	Mexican artist
a ruler	Napoleon	Napoleonic period
a city	Paris	Parisian styles
a poet	Dante	Dantean verses

Some proper nouns consist of more than one word. In these names, short prepositions (generally fewer than five letters) and articles are not capitalized.

EXAMPLES   Statue of Liberty   Alexander the Great

NOTE   Proper nouns and adjectives sometimes lose their capitals through frequent usage.

EXAMPLES   china   pasteurize   sandwich

EXERCISE 3   Identifying Correct Capitalization

For each of the following pairs of phrases, write the letter of the correct phrase on the line provided.

EX. _____ 1. a.   visit a University
                 b.   visit Stanford University

_____ 1. a.   last tuesday   _____ 3. a.   Kanes county
              b.   last Tuesday   b.   Kanes County

_____ 2. a.   the Brooklyn Bridge   _____ 4. a.   Mississippi River
              b.   a Bridge in New York City   b.   Mississippi river

_____ 5. a. a european tour   _____ 8. a. nation's laws
        b. a trip through Europe   b. mexican laws

_____ 6. a. a famous film actor   _____ 9. a. Cajun dishes
        b. actor danny glover   b. cajun dishes

_____ 7. a. a man named Eric the Red   _____ 10. a. World Trade Center
        b. a man named Eric The Red   b. World Trade center

EXERCISE 4   Correcting Errors in Capitalization

In the sentences below, underline each error in capitalization. Write your correction in the space above the error.

                October   _New York City_
EX. 1. Last <u>october</u>, my brother Earl and I went to <u>new york city</u>.

1. We took a bus from newark, new jersey, after lunch.

2. When we arrived at the greyhound station, we took another bus.

3. The bus went to Central park.

4. Sharika led the group of canadian tourists through the egyptian exhibit at the museum.

5. Many people were dressed in the latest italian styles.

6. We got off the bus and walked to lexington avenue.

7. On the way, we stopped to talk with a man called binti, an African Artist.

8. He had recently arrived from zanzibar, an island off the coast of africa.

9. He was selling persian rugs and tapestries.

10. The rugs had pictures of the united nations seal.

11. Every ten years, the bureau of the census counts the U.S. population.

12. Tagalog is the language used by the austronesian people of the same name.

13. The ukrainian Sculptor archipenko was born in 1887.

14. The Lammermuir hills are in the borders and lothian regions of Scotland.

15. Laos, formerly a state of french indochina, is in southeast Asia.

PEOPLE AND PLACES

10d **Capitalize the names of people.**

EXAMPLES   Maya Angelou, Herman Melville, Joyce Chen, Eva Perón

10e **Capitalize geographical names.**

Type of Name	Examples
continents	South America, Australia
countries	Sri Lanka, Israel, Albania
cities, towns	Oklahoma City, Acton
counties, townships	Essex County, Niles Township
states	Arizona, North Carolina
islands	Staten Island, Key West
bodies of water	Bay of Fundy, Pacific Ocean
streets, highways	South Marshall Street, Ford Boulevard
parks and forests	Natchez National Park, Sherwood Forest
mountains	Andes Mountains, Mount Everest
regions	the South, the Northwest

NOTE   Words such as *east, west, north*, and *south* are not capitalized when they indicate directions.

EXAMPLES   Drive **south** two miles and take a left. [direction]
Citrus fruits grow throughout the **South**. [region]

However, these words are capitalized when they name a particular place.

EXAMPLES   in the **N**orthwest   by the **S**outh

NOTE   In a hyphenated street number, the second part of the number is not capitalized.

EXAMPLE   West Ninety-**t**hird Street

EXERCISE 5   Correcting Errors in Capitalization

In the sentences below, underline each error in capitalization. Write your correction in the space above the error.

             Appalachian Mountains   *Georgia   Maine*

EX.   1.   The <u>appalachian mountains</u> stretch from <u>georgia</u> to <u>maine</u>.

1.   The country of argentina is in the southern part of south america.

2.   Just South of the city of new orleans, the mississippi river empties into the Gulf of Mexico.

3.   The novelist jorge amado was born in brazil in 1912.

4.   We traveled to the southwest to study the varieties of cactus that grow there.

5.   When the bus reaches herald square, how much farther will I ride to Thirty-Fifth Street?

6.   As you know, cochise was a famous American indian.

7.   The hetch hetchy valley is located in yosemite national park.

8.   Mountains known as the alps tower over much of europe.

9.   The states of new jersey and pennsylvania are separated by the delaware river.

10.   We visited my friend Ramón in jefferson city, the capital of missouri.

11.   Why did we count fifteen streets between Eleventh Street and Twenty-First Street?

12.   Penzance is a port in cornwall in the southwest part of England.

13.   The urubamba river, flowing through peru, joins a second river to become the Ucayali River.

14.   Have you ever visited the Dinaric alps Northeast of Italy?

15.   The Little Karroo mountains are part of the Drakensburg mountains in south africa.

GROUPS, EVENTS, AND NATIONALITIES

10f   Capitalize the names of organizations, teams, businesses, institutions, and government bodies.

Type of Name	Examples
organizations	American Legion
teams	Houston Oilers
businesses	Ford Motor Company
government bodies	Department of Agriculture
institutions	University of Rochester

NOTE   Do not capitalize words such as *hotel, theater, college, high school, post office,* and *courthouse* unless they are part of a proper name.

EXAMPLES   Gloucester High School
my high school

10g   Capitalize the names of historical events and periods, special events, and calendar items.

Type of Name	Examples
historical events, periods	World War I, Middle Ages
special events	Olympic Games, Summerfest
calendar items	Monday, May, Arbor Day

NOTE   Do not capitalize the name of a season unless it is personified or used in the name of a special event.

EXAMPLES   We felt Winter's rule.
the annual Dartmouth Winter Carnival

10h   Capitalize the names of nationalities, races, and peoples.

EXAMPLES   Spanish, Caucasian, Asian, Cherokee, Zulu

NOTE   The words *black* and *white* may or may not be capitalized when they refer to races.

EXAMPLE   Both Blacks and Whites [*or* blacks and whites] have worked to protect our civil rights.

EXERCISE 6   Proofreading Sentences for Correct Capitalization

In the sentences below, underline each error in capitalization. Write your correction in the space above the error.

Johnson   Bell Telephone

EX. 1. My neighbor, Mr. <u>johnson</u>, works for <u>bell</u> <u>telephone</u>.

1.   Our local bank, first federal savings, is closed on thanksgiving day.

2.   Many doctors belong to the American medical association.

3.   One well-known egyptian leader was anwar sadat.

4.   People celebrated the end of world war I on armistice day.

5.   After he graduated from the university of maryland, John Lucas played basketball for the houston rockets.

6.   The Veterans of Foreign Wars helps soldiers from world wars I and II.

7.   In Canada, Christmas day is the day before Boxing day.

8.   Among Spanish leaders of the Middle ages, el cid was quite famous.

9.   We gladly said farewell to summer and her long, hot days.

10.   Fans throughout the stadium cheered the team from the university of arizona.

EXERCISE 7   Identifying Correct Capitalization

For each of the pairs of phrases below, write the letter of the correct phrase on the line provided.

EX. _____*a.*_____ 1.   a.   the Chicago Bulls
                         b.   the New York mets

_____   1.   a.   a pleasant stay at the Bellevue hotel
                 b.   a pleasant stay at the Bellevue Hotel

_____   2.   a.   a Service Bureau
                 b.   the Internal Revenue Service

_____   3.   a.   an Italian opera
                 b.   a french artist

_____   4.   a.   raced in the New York City Marathon
                 b.   raced in the Marathon

_____   5.   a.   Stone age humans
                 b.   Iron Age humans

MODULE 10: CAPITAL LETTERS

OBJECT, STRUCTURES, AND SCHOOL SUBJECTS

10i **Capitalize brand names and trade names.**

EXAMPLES   Chicken of the Sea, Apple, Xerox

NOTE   Do not capitalize a common noun that follows a brand name: Chicken of the Sea tuna, Apple computer.

10j **Capitalize the names of ships, monuments, awards, planets, and other particular places or things.**

Type of Name	Examples
ships, trains	the *Mayflower*, the *Orient Express*
aircraft, spacecraft, missiles	*Hindenburg, Apollo I, Patriot*
monuments, memorials	Bunker Hill Monument, Martin Luther King, Jr., Memorial Center
buildings	Town Hall, Lincoln Center
awards	Nobel Prize
planets, stars	Mercury, the North Star

10k **Do not capitalize names of school subjects, except for languages or course names followed by a number.**

EXAMPLE   Besides math and art, I'm taking Italian and History 102.

EXERCISE 8   Proofreading Sentences for Correct Capitalization

In the following sentences, underline each error in capitalization. Write your correction in the space above the error.

Apple
EX.   1. Our school recently bought <u>apple</u> computers.

1.   The *Spirit of st. louis* was Charles Lindbergh's Airplane.

2.   The Passenger Ship named *titanic* struck an iceberg.

3.   Did *Gone with the Wind*, the famous movie that was set during the american civil war, win an academy award?

4.   I am giving my sister a timex watch for Graduation.

5. The First Star you see at night is often the planet venus.

6. Roberto has to choose between Algebra II and American History.

7. Did the spacecraft called *skylab* travel to any Planets?

8. When you're in washington, d.c., be sure to visit the white house and the vietnam veterans war memorial.

9. The french novelist Jules Verne wrote about a fictitious submarine called *nautilus*, piloted by Captain nemo.

10. The Poet Richard Wilbur won the pulitzer prize in 1957 and in 1989.

11. Have you checked the records on file at city hall?

12. Scientists wonder what the environments of saturn and pluto might be like.

13. Did Rayjean tell you the old joke about who is buried in grant's tomb?

14. The Bay area rapid transit system helps workers get to their jobs.

15. Chuck won the most valuable player award again this year.

EXERCISE 9   Writing Sentences Using Correct Capitalization

You are a reporter covering the International Trade Fair in Tokyo, Japan. You are writing down notes that you can later use in an article. On your own paper, write ten sentences. In your sentences, include at least two of the rules for capitalization covered in this lesson. You might include types of products, companies represented, and awards won.

EX. 1. *The U.S. Waterbed Co. won the Most Unusual New Product Award for its collapsible waterbed.*

MODULE 10: CAPITAL LETTERS

TITLES

10l   **Capitalize titles.**

(1)   Capitalize the title of a person when it comes before a name.

EXAMPLES   **D**r. Schweitzer, **S**enator Boxer, **M**s. Katz

Do not capitalize a title that is used alone or that follows a person's name. Often, these titles are preceded by *a* or *the*.

EXAMPLES   A **p**resident whom I admire was Abraham Lincoln.
My friend Samantha is **v**ice-**p**resident of the Stamp Club.

When a title is used alone in a direct address, it is usually capitalized.

EXAMPLES   I would like to interview you, **S**enator. Thanks, **D**octor.

EXCEPTIONS   Yes, **S**ir [or sir]. I will, **M**a'am [or ma'am].

(2)   Capitalize words showing family relationship when used with a person's name, but *not* when preceded by a possessive.

EXAMPLES   **G**randmother Smith **A**unt Tanya my **g**randfather your **f**ather

(3)   Capitalize the first and last words and all important words in titles of books, periodicals, poems, stories, historical documents, movies, television programs, works of art, and short musical compositions.

Unimportant words in titles include articles (*a, an, the*), coordinating conjunctions (*and, but, for, nor, or, so, yet*), and prepositions of fewer than five letters (*by, for, on, with*).

Type of Name	Examples
books	*A Tale of Two Cities*
periodicals	the *Chicago Tribune*
poems	"The Hollow Men"
stories	"The Open Window"
historical documents	Bill of Rights
movies	*Mary Poppins Returns*
television programs	*America's Funniest Home Videos*
works of art	*View of Toledo*
short musical works	"A Minor Variation"

EXERCISE 10   Proofreading Sentences for Correct Capitalization

In the sentences below, underline each error in capitalization. Write your correction in the space above the error.

Rolling Stone

EX.   1. Annie Lennox was interviewed in that issue of <u>*rolling stone*</u>.

1.   In 2012, governor Mitt Romney lost the election to president Barack Obama.

2.   Uncle dan gave me a copy of Dorothy Parker's story, "a telephone call."

3.   I read a review of Tom Clancy's book, *under fire*, in the Sunday paper.

4.   My Cousin Adrienne and I have learned to play Willie Nelson's song "stranger" on the piano.

5.   I got interested in poetry only after I read "break, break, break" by Tennyson.

6.   "I gave it to your Father," said professor Jones.

7.   Let's get the march issue of *harper's*.

8.   I don't remember who wrote the declaration of independence, but I know that john hancock signed it.

9.   constable's painting *wivenhoe park, essex* is of the actual Wivenhoe Park.

10.   My Mother hopes to write a book called *cooking for others*, about her days at *La Cantina*.

11.   Have they read any of the books by doctor Joyce Brothers?

12.   Please ask Gerry to find out how many Presidents have been elected since 1900.

13.   King john of england did not want to sign the magna carta.

14.   Grandma moses painted *Out for Christmas trees* in 1987.

15.   The musical *Sunday In The Park With George* is based on the life of the French painter Georges Seurat.

MODULE REVIEW

A. Correcting Errors in Capitalization

In the sentences below, underline each error in capitalization. Write your correction in the space above the error.

                    I   *high school*   *Allegheny College*
EX.   1.   When i finish High School, I want to go to allegheny college.

1.   Yes, doctor, i did read the article about you in *the denver post.*

2.   The japanese city of hiroshima is located on a large Bay.

3.   In philadelphia, the franklin institute is on benjamin franklin parkway.

4.   Ana's Uncle Georgio wrote an article about the Spacecraft *challenger.*

5.   When you're in the northwest, be sure to visit the city of seattle.

6.   candace bergen, a television star, spoke at the spring women's conference at the University where my aunt Flo teaches.

7.   We received a letter from governor rick perry of texas.

8.   I bought this perdue chicken at hal's market on Fifty-Third Street.

9.   Was this house really the inspiration for Nathaniel Hawthorne's book *the house of the seven gables?*

10.   My Grandmother always says, "Waste not, want not."

11.   Shall I take Biology I, English I, or Algebra?

12.   West Indian music combines African, spanish, and other styles.

13.   The National science fair is scheduled for early in the winter.

14.   Marlene's new poem begins, "Say, Let me tell you a story."

15.   Is Thanksgiving day always celebrated on a thursday ?

B. Proofreading a Paragraph for Correct Capitalization

In the paragraph below, all capital letters have been omitted. Underline each word that should be capitalized. Write your correction in the space above the word.

                Next Tuesday   *West Chester Junior High*   *Earth Day*
EX.   [1] next tuesday the students at west chester junior high will celebrate earth day.

[1] my friend bobby ray robinson and i are making an exhibit called "steel from trash." [2] last week, we drove east on route 30 to interview doctor ramón martínez of the lukens steel company in the city of coatesville. [3] he assured us that his company is very interested in purchasing clean, used steel cans from the residents of west chester. [4] when bobby ray heard that, he said, "Let's get this recycling project off the ground!" [5] we are thinking about writing a letter to the *west chester gazette.*

C. Working with a Partner to Report on a Space Journey

The year is 2110, and you and your partner are newspaper reporters. Your editor has asked you to accompany an astronaut as she journeys into space. The purpose of your trip is to interview the astronaut, gathering details about her childhood and education, her training as an astronaut, the goals of her mission, and her hopes for the future.

1. Working together, use the internet to make notes about current space missions. Add science fiction details to put your journey clearly into future times. Create character details for the astronaut. What might she have studied in school? How might she have trained for this mission?

2. On your own paper, write a news story based on your notes. Identify the name of the spacecraft, the name of the astronaut's school and hometown, the astronaut's cultural background, and the planets or stars the astronaut plans to visit. Be sure to capitalize correctly.

3. Be sure to include the name of your newspaper and your editor.

EX. *Astronaut June Villarmo is proof of how important Science 102 can be!*

MODULE 11: PUNCTUATION

END MARKS AND ABBREVIATIONS

End marks are used to show the purpose of a sentence.

11a   **A period follows a statement (or declarative sentence).**

EXAMPLE   My father speaks Yiddish fluently.

11b   **A question mark follows a question (or interrogative sentence).**

EXAMPLE   Can you open this jar?

11c   **An exclamation point follows an exclamation.**

EXAMPLE   What a terrible storm that was!

11d   **Either a period or an exclamation point may follow an imperative sentence.**

EXAMPLES   Please wait here. [a request]
Don't touch that! [a command]

11e   **A period usually follows an abbreviation.**

Abbreviations with Periods	
Personal Names	I. M. Pei, H. H. Munroe
Titles Used with Names	Mrs., Ms., Mr., Dr., Jr., Sr.
Organizations and Companies	Co., Inc., Assn.
Addresses	St., Rd., Ave., P.O. Box
Times	A.M., P.M., B.C., A.D.
Abbreviations Without Periods	
Government Agencies	HUD, IRS, FBI, WHO
States followed by ZIP Codes	Encinitas, CA 92024
Units of Measure	mg, cm, g, pt, gal, lb
Other Organizations	NASA, YMCA, NAACP

EXERCISE 1   Adding End Marks to Sentences

Write the end mark that should appear at the end of each sentence below.

EX.   1.   On what day does the Vietnamese holiday Tet begin*?*

1.   We will be fine if the rain doesn't start
2.   How wonderful it is to meet you at last
3.   Where do you leave newspapers for recycling
4.   Tamara will proofread my book report
5.   Were those pots made by a Maricopa potter
6.   Please hold the door for me
7.   How can we fix this bicycle
8.   Stop that noise immediately
9.   What a great interview Laurence Yep gave
10.   This dog doesn't seem to have a license or rabies tag
11.   Which museum will we visit on this field trip
12.   Return these books to the library, please
13.   A seismograph records earthquake data
14.   Don't jump off a seesaw too quickly
15.   Why can't we go to lunch together

EXERCISE 2   Proofreading for the Correct Use of Abbreviations

Add or delete periods where needed in the items below. On the line before each name or phrase, write *C* if the name or phrase is correct.

EX.   _____   1. Mrs. Violette A. Johnson

_____   1.   is 12 cm. long
_____   2.   at 311 Catalpa Dr
_____   3.   U S Senator Joseph Montoya
_____   4.   Ed Begley, Jr
_____   5.   West Warwick, RI 02893
_____   6.   inside FBI headquarters
_____   7.   weighs 6 g
_____   8.   at 2:30 AM
_____   9.   E L Baines Enterprises, Inc
_____   10. the room is 6 ft 6 in long

_____   11. Dr Laura Stans
_____   12. in the third century BC
_____   13. Juan Sánchez, Sr.
_____   14. by 3:00 P.M.
_____   15. Ms. J R Peale
_____   16. with the I.R.S.
_____   17. Brooklyn, NY
_____   18. San Diego, CA 92119
_____   19. 18 mg.
_____   20. PO Box 87

COMMAS IN A SERIES

11f   Use commas to separate items in a series.

EXAMPLES   I will have hummus, tahini, and pita bread. [words]
They found locusts in their car, on their porch, and even in their kitchen. [phrases]
The drawings that Tena had dreamed about, that she had struggled to create, and that she had carefully matted were sold in a week. [clauses]

(1)   If all items in a series are joined by *and* or *or*, do not use commas to separate them.

EXAMPLE   The bronco kicked and bucked and reared.

(2)   Semicolons usually separate independent clauses in a series. Commas may separate short independent clauses, however.

EXAMPLES   We arrived well before dawn; we scrubbed the walls and ceilings; and we painted the rooms a pale blue.
We arrived, we cleaned, and we painted.

11g   Use commas to separate two or more adjectives preceding a noun.

EXAMPLE   This sari is a fine, beautiful silk.

When the last adjective in a series is thought of as part of the noun, the comma before the adjective is omitted. Compound nouns like *orange juice* and *lunch box* are considered single units.

EXAMPLE   My father grabbed his steel lunch box.

NOTE   Try inserting *and* between the adjectives in a series. If *and* fits sensibly, use a comma. For example, *fine and beautiful* sounds sensible, so a comma is used. *And* cannot be logically inserted in *steel lunch box*, however.

EXERCISE 3   Proofreading Sentences for the Correct Use of Commas

Add commas where needed in the following sentences. On the line before each sentence, write *C* if the sentence is correct.

EX. _____   1.   We rode through forests, up mountains, and across a desert.

_____   1.   French, Spanish and German will be offered next year.

_____ 2. Look for shrubs that are short rounded and dense.

_____ 3. Duane stared across the vast cornfields.

_____ 4. Invite Tyree to sing to dance or to tell jokes.

_____ 5. Jennifer sputtered coughed and finally took a deep breath.

_____ 6. Heat drought and poor soil were our biggest obstacles.

_____ 7. Someone drove up saw your sign and left a dollar.

_____ 8. We invited all of our aunts uncles and cousins.

_____ 9. Aretha was so determined to find her ring that she searched in the house in the yard and even out in the orchard.

_____ 10. Our bus soon began to produce clouds of black greasy smoke.

_____ 11. The poets that we studied included Robert Frost and Zora Neale Hurston.

_____ 12. The salsa that my mother makes is thick red and spicy.

_____ 13. You would have time to visit São Paulo stop in Rio de Janeiro and still meet your cousin in Recife.

_____ 14. All you have to do is nod and smile and keep quiet.

_____ 15. People write from right to left in Egypt Iran and Israel.

_____ 16. We sat on the metal fire escape to enjoy the cool air.

_____ 17. That character has appeared in books plays poems and films.

_____ 18. This is a person who is honest fearless and admired.

_____ 19. Shanghai seemed stylish successful and busy when we visited last year.

_____ 20. Postcards books and magazines are for sale in this store.

MODULE 11: PUNCTUATION

COMMAS WITH COMPOUND SENTENCES

11h	**Use commas before *and, but, for, or, nor, so*, and *yet* when they join independent clauses.**

EXAMPLE   Chico dove for the ball**, but** Shing reached it first.

NOTE   A comma is always used before *for, so*, and *yet* when they join two independent clauses. The comma may be omitted, however, when the independent clauses are very short; before *and, but, or* or *nor;* and when there is no possibility of misunderstanding.

EXAMPLE   Dad washed and I dried.

Do not be misled by compound verbs, which often make a sentence look as if it contains two independent clauses.

SIMPLE SENTENCE   Lian **sharpened** her pencil and **sat** down to write.
[one subject with a compound verb]

COMPOUND SENTENCE   First Lian sharpened her pencil**, and** then she began to write.
[two independent clauses]

EXERCISE 4   Correcting Compound Sentences by Adding Commas

For each of the following sentences, add commas where needed. On the line before the sentence, write *C* if the sentence is correct.

EX.   _*C*_   1. Amy climbed on her horse, but then she had to wait for us.

_____   1.   The falafel contained no meat yet it was very filling.

_____   2.   A dark cloud approached from the east and gradually filled up the sky.

_____   3.   The river was crowded for today was market day.

_____   4.   The first pictures of Venus came in and they were startling.

_____   5.   You can read for an hour or you can make the salad.

_____   6.   Amy could not even see her hand nor could she find the light switch.

_____   7.   Before the show started, Chad climbed on stage and tested the microphones.

_____   8.   I wasn't wearing repellent yet the mosquitoes didn't bite me.

_____ 9. Neither my cousin in Ohio nor my cousin in Texas drives yet.

_____ 10. The calendar is very old and it is made of stone.

_____ 11. How far did you have to go for the milk and eggs?

_____ 12. We haven't started school yet but we will begin on Monday.

_____ 13. Charlotte laughed but I didn't.

_____ 14. Douglas lost his dollar so he had to go home.

_____ 15. The sign said we had to pay ten dollars but the woman at the gate let us in for free.

EXERCISE 5   Combining Sentences

On your own paper, rewrite each pair of sentences as a single compound sentence. Use a comma and *and, but, for, nor, or, so,* or *yet.*

EX. 1. We could go to a movie. We could rent one.
   1. *We could go to a movie, or we could rent one.*

1. We can go to the station now. The bus doesn't leave for two hours.

2. I swam for hours. I wasn't tired.

3. The fiesta began on Thursday. It continued for three days.

4. I studied hard for this quiz. I am as ready as I can be.

5. Most dogs aren't allowed in here. Guide dogs are always welcome.

6. I fed that plant and watered it. It still won't grow.

7. Long ago, that woman died of smallpox. She wasn't allowed to be buried with the other townspeople.

8. Some beads were made of shell. These are made of bone.

9. Put the spoiled food in the compost heap. Grind it up in the disposal.

10. This letter is very fragile. It was written almost two hundred years ago.

11. We left the party early. We were not having fun.

12. Put covers on your textbooks. They will stay clean.

13. Volunteers stacked sandbags along the riverbank. The river flowed over the sandbags.

14. Maxine was our best hockey player. She wanted to try out for the track team.

15. Roland likes apples. Abby prefers peaches.

COMMAS WITH NONESSENTIAL WORDS

11i **Use commas to set off nonessential clauses and nonessential participial phrases.**

A *nonessential* (or *nonrestrictive*) clause or participial phrase adds information that is not necessary to the main idea in the sentence.

NONESSENTIAL PHRASE   The cook, **smiling broadly,** bowed at us.

NONESSENTIAL CLAUSE   This fabric, **which is tie-dyed,** came from East Africa.

When a clause or phrase is necessary to the meaning of a sentence—that is, when it tells *which one*—the clause or phrase is *essential* (or *restrictive*), and commas are not used.

ESSENTIAL PHRASE   The car **sitting on the trailer** is a dragster. [*Which* car?]

ESSENTIAL CLAUSE   The book **that I reserved** is for a report. [*Which* book?]

NOTE   An adjective clause beginning with *that* is usually essential.

EXERCISE 6   Using Commas Correctly

On the line before each sentence, identify each italicized phrase or clause by writing *e.* for *essential* or *n.e.* for *nonessential*. Insert commas where necessary.

EX.   _n.e._   1.   The speech was by Chief Joseph, a Nez Perce chief.

_____   1.   This manuscript *which is very old* belongs in a museum.

_____   2.   The kimchi *that Bob makes* is spicier than mine.

_____   3.   Don't you wonder why that diamond *lost for centuries* should suddenly turn up here?

_____   4.   The mural *that you liked* was painted by Diego Rivera.

_____   5.   Lobster Newburg *which was named for a man named Wenberg* is made with a delicious sauce.

_____   6.   This little menorah is the one *that we light during Hanukkah.*

_____   7.   Ricardo owns a brown-and-white horse *which looks like an appaloosa to me.*

_____   8.   Circle any words *that you don't understand.*

_____   9.   Geothermal energy *already popular in Denmark* is gradually finding supporters in the United States.

_____ 10. The woman *on the camel* is a Mongolian sheepherder.

_____ 11. Juan de la Cierva is one of the two men *who perfected the helicopter.*

_____ 12. The biography Hidden Figures *which was written by Margot Lee Shetterly* was made into a movie.

_____ 13. A band of dust *which some scientists blame on the eruption of Mt. Pinatubo* is now circling the globe.

_____ 14. The large dog *on the right* is a Great Dane.

_____ 15. Labor Day *which the Mexicans celebrate on May 1* is a festive holiday.

_____ 16. The Braille alphabet *which consists of patterns of raised dots* was named for its inventor.

_____ 17. The statue shows Thomas Gallaudet *for whom Gallaudet College is named.*

_____ 18. Millions of people perished as a result of the Black Death *which was a form of bubonic plague.*

_____ 19. Early hockey teams *playing on frozen lakes* sometimes had thirty players on a team.

_____ 20. The lucky astronauts were the ones *who rode in Apollo 11.*

_____ 21. Nancy lives next door to the new recreation center *which is made of red brick.*

_____ 22. Turn the handle *attached to the left side* to operate the jack-in-the-box.

_____ 23. A jaguar is a fierce forest cat *resembling a leopard.*

_____ 24. Professor Dunlap *who teaches driver safety* is originally from New Hampshire.

_____ 25. Quicksand will quickly swallow any heavy object *falling into it.*

COMMAS WITH INTRODUCTORY WORDS

11j Use a comma after words such as *well, yes, no,* and *why* when they begin a sentence.

EXAMPLES **No,** we won't be late.
Well, it's finally finished.

11k Use a comma after an introductory participial phrase.

EXAMPLE **Jumping up,** Carlotta grabbed the ball.

11l Use a comma after a series of introductory prepositional phrases.

A short introductory prepositional phrase does not require a comma unless the comma is necessary to make the meaning clear.

EXAMPLES **In the front of the store,** two clerks were ringing up purchases.
After dinner we talked for hours.
After dinner, time seemed to stand still. [The comma is needed to avoid reading *"dinner time"*]

11m Use a comma after an introductory adverb clause.

EXAMPLES **When you're finished,** please help me here.

11n Use commas to separate items in dates and addresses.

EXAMPLES On **September 5, 1968,** a star was born!
I will be at **54 Howard Lane, Bartow, FL 33830.**

11o Use a comma after the salutation of a friendly letter and after the closing of any letter.

EXAMPLES Dear Ms. Hoy,   Sincerely yours,

11p Use a comma after a name followed by an abbreviation such as Jr., Sr., and M.D.

EXAMPLES Martin Luther King, Jr.   Ben Casey, M.D.

EXERCISE 7   Adding Commas with Introductory Elements

In each of the following sentences, add commas where needed. On the line before the sentence, write *C* if the sentence is correct.

EX. _____ 1. Washing my clothes in the river, I saw an alligator.

_____ 1. In the back of the closet Jared noticed a small door.

_____ 2. Yes the writer Miguel Angel Asturias did win a Nobel Prize.

_____ 3. Singing at the top of her lungs Heather attracted quite a bit of attention.

_____ 4. Before you leave, look at this picture of Lou Gehrig.

_____ 5. As you read the module ask yourself questions about it.

_____ 6. Next to the kayak a much larger boat was being built.

_____ 7. At noon everyone took a short break for lunch.

_____ 8. Climbing over the fence Guido noticed a nest of rabbits.

_____ 9. Before you lock up check the alarm system.

_____ 10. Why one of my friends made it for me.

_____ 11. Say do you know Frieda?

_____ 12. Because Mother worked all day, she is tired tonight.

_____ 13. However we know that you did the best job that you could.

_____ 14. At the sound of the bell everyone should leave the building.

_____ 15. Why do onions make a person's eyes water?

EXERCISE 8 Using Commas Correctly

On your own paper, rewrite the sentences below, inserting commas where needed.

EX. 1. March 9 2018 was a truly memorable day.

1. *March 9, 2018, was a truly memorable day.*

1. On September 9 1957 Congress established the Commission on Civil Rights.

2. A terrible blizzard struck New York City on March 11 1888.

3. In a letter to the editor of our school paper Duncan wrote about our lunchroom schedule.

4. You can write to the American Hockey League at 1425 Cypress Hill Avenue Springfield MA 01089.

5. After we moved into our new house we met our neighbor Harriet Barlow Ph.D.

6. This note arrived yesterday: "Dear Aunt Jo Thanks. Kisses Kim."

7. I need the address of Fran Ahola M.D. of Dayton Ohio.

8. On April 7 1992 Debra began her job as office assistant.

9. Wow what an exciting concert that was last night!

10. Why is the date May 28 2015 important to your mother?

COMMAS WITH SENTENCE INTERRUPTERS

11q **Use commas to set off elements that interrupt the sentence.**

Two commas are used around an interrupting element—one before the "interrupter" and one after. If the interrupter comes at the beginning or the end of the sentence, only one comma is needed.

EXAMPLES   Roberto Clemente, **the ball player,** once lived there.
Furthermore, the whales are protected.
I need some help, **Kai.**

(1) Appositives and appositive phrases are usually set off by commas.

EXAMPLES   Inez, **my pen pal,** is an artist.
The documentary told about spelunkers, **people who explore caves for a hobby.**

If an appositive is closely related to the word preceding it, it should not be set off by commas.

EXAMPLE   I am looking for my friend **Greg.**

(2) Words used in direct address are set off by commas.

EXAMPLES   **Mrs. Ignacio,** your cab is here.
I know, **Mai,** that you will do your best.
We want to thank you, **Jolon.**

(3) Parenthetical expressions are set off by commas.

Parenthetical expressions are side remarks that add information or relate ideas.

EXAMPLES   The bronze lion, **in fact,** is quite common.
For instance, look at this butterfly.

EXERCISE 9   Proofreading Sentences for the Correct Use of Commas

For each of the following sentences, underline the appositive word or phrase. Add commas where needed.

EX.   1.   The animal, <u>a guanaco,</u> is related to the camel.

1.   My sister Kate knows all about camels and guanacos.

2.   East of the Andes a mountain range in South America live the guanacos.

3. Another relative of the camel the alpaca is also used for wool.

4. Alpacas descendants of the guanaco are bred for their wool.

5. The bigger animals the llamas are becoming popular pets.

6. Llama wool a very coarse fiber is used for making rope.

7. Llamas sturdy animals are also used as pack animals.

8. The country that I visited Peru still uses llamas.

9. Another pack animal the dromedary lives in Asia and Africa.

10. Dromedaries the camels with one hump can carry heavy loads.

EXERCISE 10 Punctuating Sentence Interrupters

In the sentences below, add commas where needed.

EX.   1. Mah-jong, I believe, is an ancient game.

1. To be honest I never understood the appeal.

2. Please tell me what you think Ms. Karas.

3. My grandmother for example loved her sports car.

4. Uncle Marco do you remember the 1970s?

5. The beauty of the orchid I suppose isn't in its scent.

6. By the way did everyone in the 1920s love jazz?

7. I understand Keiko that you want a new kimono.

8. Nevertheless I refuse to use pesticide.

9. *Alice in Wonderland* was written in English; it has however been translated into many other languages.

10. Like all fads of course pet rocks lost popularity.

11. Toni Morrison my favorite author won the Nobel Prize in literature in 1993.

12. At any rate a majority of the senators will vote to pass the legislation.

13. One of these days Marcia we must find your jacket.

14. What happened at the end of the movie Dennis?

15. My aunt Mae an avid gardener loves her roses.

A. Proofreading Sentences for Correct Use of Commas

In the sentences below, insert commas where needed.

EX. 1. Caves, after all, can be rich sources of history.

1. I have visited caves in Virginia Pennsylvania and Kentucky.

2. In some caves scientists have found traces of ancient tools.

3. Thousands of years before Columbus arrived people were living in North American caves.

4. Scientists have found these caves and sometimes people discover tools inside them.

5. Some caves had walls some had roofs and some had separate rooms.

6. The tools which were made of stone were buried in the dirt.

7. They were preserved naturally by the hot dry air.

8. In limestone caves in the Southwest archaeologists even found mummies.

9. In one cave pet dogs were found buried next to bones.

10. Indeed these early people had baskets blankets and pets.

B. Proofreading a Paragraph for Correct Use of Commas

In the following paragraph, insert commas where needed.

EX. [1] This park, I think, was designed by Olmsted.

[1] Frederick Law Olmsted was born on April 26 1882. [2] He began life in Hartford Connecticut. [3] He went to college at Yale University and he studied agriculture and engineering. [4] After he graduated he traveled through Europe to study gardens. [5] When he returned he became both the architect and the superintendent of Central Park in New York City. [6] He went on to design parks in Boston Chicago Detroit and Montreal. [7] Why did you know that the University of California in Berkeley California had Olmsted design its campus? [8] It is certainly a

beautiful place. [9] Olmsted's son another Frederick also designed parks. [10] In fact he designed a whole system of parks for Boston Massachusetts.

C.   Writing Brief Descriptions

You are writing to someone your age who is moving to your area. This person will be attending your school. You have included a list of some of the activities and clubs available at school that you think this person would like to know about. Write brief descriptions of four of these activities or clubs.

1.   First, choose four school activities or clubs.

2.   Choose three details about each of them. Write at least two sentences about each activity or club, and use at least one comma in each sentence.

EX.   1.   *One club you might like, the Chess Club, meets twice a month.*

1. _____

_____

_____

_____

2. _____

_____

_____

_____

3. _____

_____

_____

_____

4. _____

_____

_____

_____

MODULE 11: PUNCTUATION

SEMICOLONS

11r Use a semicolon between independent clauses if they are not joined by *and, but, or, nor, for, so,* or *yet.*

EXAMPLES Selma pressed the button and waited**;** nothing happened.
Our bathroom leads a double life**;** it's also a darkroom.

11s Use a semicolon between independent clauses joined by conjunctive adverbs or transitional expressions.

Commonly Used Conjunctive Adverbs			
accordingly	furthermore	meanwhile	otherwise
also	however	moreover	still
besides	indeed	nevertheless	then
consequently	instead	next	therefore
Commonly Used Transitional Expressions			
as a result	for instance	in fact	on the other hand
for example	in addition	in other words	that is

EXAMPLES I have a cat**; therefore,** I have cat hair on my clothes much of the time.
Stacking wood is no fun**; on the other hand,** it is good exercise.

11t A semicolon (rather than a comma) may be needed to separate independent clauses joined by a coordinating conjunction when there are commas within the clauses.

CONFUSING You must bring boots, socks, and a backpack, but fruit, nuts, and a cup would be nice.

CLEAR You must bring boots, socks, and a backpack**;** but fruit, nuts, and a cup would be nice.

11u Use a semicolon between items in a series if the items contain commas.

EXAMPLE I have lived in Beaufort, North Carolina**;** New Orleans, Louisiana**;** Evanston, Illinois**;** and Gloucester, Massachusetts.

EXERCISE 11 Using Semicolons Correctly

In each sentence below, add the missing semicolon.

EX. 1. The flag of the United States has fifty stars; each star stands for a state.

1. Almost everyone recognizes our country's flag however, few recognize our state's flag.

2. All states have flags some are quite beautiful.

3. Some have pictures on them the flag of California, for example, shows a bear.

4. Arkansas was our twenty-fifth state as a result, its flag has twenty-five white stars on it to show the states.

5. The Arkansas flag is red, white, and blue and it has three blue stars beneath the name *Arkansas* representing Spain, France, and the United States.

6. Texas has had many flags flown over it at one point France, Spain, and Mexico all claimed it.

7. Ohio's flag is different from other flags it is swallow-tailed instead of rectangular.

8. The Ohio flag's stripes represent roads and waterways its stars represent the original states and its circle represents the Northwest Territory.

9. The flag of West Virginia shows a wreath of rhododendron, the state flower a cap of liberty and a ribbon with the state name.

10. The American Legion in Alaska sponsored a flag-design contest Benny Benson, from the Jesse Lee Mission Home, was the winner.

11. This thirteen-year-old boy designed Alaska's flag the flag shows the constellation known as the Big Dipper.

12. Alaska became the forty-ninth state on January 3 the year was 1959.

13. Michigan and Arkansas became states at the same time on the Arkansas flag, a pair of stars on the blue band represents this relationship.

14. Some flags use stars to show that they were once territories others use circles.

15. The state of Washington was named for George Washington he was our first president.

11v Use a colon to mean "note what follows."

(1) Use a colon before a list of items, especially after expressions like *the following* and *as follows*.

EXAMPLES   Your test will contain the following items: definitions, multiple-choice questions, and two essay questions.

Please bring these when you come: two sharp pencils, a calculator, and one sheet of scratch paper.

NOTE   Do not use a colon before a list that follows a verb or a preposition.

INCORRECT   Pay special attention to: the size, the shape of the tail, and the shape of the bill.

CORRECT   Pay special attention to these features: the size, the shape of the tail, and the shape of the bill.

(2) Use a colon before a long, formal statement or a long quotation.

EXAMPLE   This is how I feel about friends: "By helping you today, I give you the chance to help me tomorrow."

11w Use a colon in certain conventional situations.

(1) Use a colon between the hour and the minute.

EXAMPLES   The film starts at 7:00 P.M.   Try to call before 10:00 A.M.

(2) Use a colon between module and verse in referring to passages from the Bible.

EXAMPLES   Genesis 43:29–34   James 3:7–11

(3) Use a colon after the salutation of a business letter.

EXAMPLES   Dear Mr. Blanco: Dear Personnel Manager:

EXERCISE 12   Adding Colons to Sentences

In each of the following sentences, add the missing colon.

EX.   1. Make sure that the names of the following cities are on your tickets: Portland, Seattle, and Vancouver.

1.   Many couples include Ruth 1 16 in their wedding ceremonies.

2. These are my favorite breakfast foods waffles, fresh fruit, and orange juice.

3. Every morning, Dad rides the 7 45 commuter train into town.

4. You will need these items before beginning bobsled training a helmet, gloves, and kneepads.

5. We will dismiss classes at 2 30 P.M. on school days before holidays.

6. We should ask these people to help with the science project David, Susan, Anna, and Tony.

7. Please write "Dear Sir or Madam" for your business letter salutation.

8. This year's transportation show includes a variety of vehicles cars, trucks, vans, and motorcycles.

9. Do you have these things on the grocery list onions, apples, paper towels, soap?

10. Mathew has appeared in two plays *The Diary of Anne Frank* and *High Noon.*

EXERCISE 13   Using Colons Correctly

Proofread the following business letter. Add, delete, or replace punctuation as necessary.

1   Dear Ms. Reynolds,

2   I am writing to confirm your speaking engagement at our church

3   on Sunday, April 10. Pastor Reeves will open the proceedings at

4   3;00 P.M. with a reading of Isaiah 40.28–31.

5   We have the following audiovisual equipment available for your

6   use, a slide projector, a VCR, and an audiocassette player. Please let

7   me know if you require any other equipment or supplies.

8   Sincerely:

9   Maureen A. Brown

A. Proofreading Sentences for Correct Use of Commas

For each of the sentences below, add commas where needed.

> EX. 1. Mary Cassatt, I heard, was an interesting woman.

1. Well she was born just before midnight on May 22 1844.

2. Shortly after that her family moved to Allegheny City Pennsylvania.

3. At the age of seven she moved to France with her family.

4. The three other children in the family were Lydia Alexander and Robert.

5. When Mary was a young woman she returned to Paris to study art.

6. She drew she painted and she met other artists.

7. Many of her early works in fact were destroyed in a fire that hit Chicago on October 8 1871.

8. One of her most famous paintings *The Bath* shows a mother bathing a child.

9. Besides working at her art Cassatt strongly supported women's rights.

10. In her later years however her eyesight failed and this failure forced her to stop painting.

B. Using End Marks, Commas, Semicolons, and Colons Correctly in a Paragraph

Add the missing punctuation to the following paragraph.

1   July 15 1993 was a red-letter day we started driving across the

2   United States For the past two years my family has talked about

3   making this trip and we finally did it On our first day we drove by

4   these cities Providence Rhode Island Hartford Connecticut Albany

5   New York and Cleveland Ohio Why did we drive so far Well we

6   had seen all these places before When we crossed the Mississippi

7   River we slowed down and started sightseeing We reached Arizona

8   my favorite state during the last week in July We all loved the state

9   indeed we stayed there two weeks Arizona has a lot to see Navajo

10   and Hopi communities Grand Canyon National Park and several

11   national monuments

C.   Proofreading a Letter

Add the missing punctuation to the business letter below.

1   5691 Blue Elm Place
2   Waverly PA 18471
3   October 10 2019
4   Dr Tonya Powell
5   4005 Willowbrook Drive
6   Bangor PA 18013
7   Dear Dr Powell
8   I understand that you are seeking volunteers for the
9   Community Supper which you hold every Wednesday evening
10   between 6 30 and 8 00 P M Our class advisor Ms Rice explained
11   your program and asked for volunteers.
12   Many students were interested consequently we can fully staff
13   the supper during the months of November December and
14   January Will you need additional volunteers after that date If you
15   will, just let us know Your volunteers for November will include
16   the following four students Margaret Lee Flavio Torres Rebecca
17   Solomon and me
18   We have all been told what to expect Dr. Powell According to
19   Ms Rice you need people to cook to serve and to clean up
20   afterward Everyone who volunteered is willing to do any of those
21   tasks, I believe We are delighted to be able to help and we look
22   forward to meeting you As you requested we will arrive at 6 15
23   the first night for an orientation tour
24   Sincerely
25   Farah Davis

(ITALICS) UNDERLINING

12a **Use italics for titles of books, plays, periodicals, films, television programs, works of art, long musical compositions, ships, aircraft, and spacecraft.**

Type of Name	Examples
Books	*The Hunger Games, A Separate Peace*
Plays	*Raisin in the Sun, Hamilton*
Periodicals	*International Herald Tribune, Smithsonian*
Films	*Casablanca, Green Book*
Television Programs	*Jeopardy, Entertainment Tonight*
Works of Art	*The Footballer, Urban Freeways*
Long Musical Compositions	*Treemonisha, Messiah*
Ships	*Titanic, Columbia*
Aircraft	*Spirit of Columbus, Air Force One*
Spacecraft	*Apollo 12, Orion*

NOTE   The article *the* is often written before a title but is not capitalized unless it is part of the official title. The official title of a book is found on the title page. The official title of a newspaper or periodical is found on the masthead, which usually appears on the editorial page.

EXAMPLE   I read the editorial in **the** *Houston Post*.

12b **Use italics for words, letters, and figures referred to as such and for foreign words.**

EXAMPLES   The words ***bite*** and ***bight*** are homophones.
The word does not have an *e* at the end.
There are two digits in ***10***.
Do you like to eat ***akara?***

EXERCISE 1 Using Italics Correctly

For each sentence below, underline the word or item that should be italicized.

EX. 1. Which actor played the policeman in the film <u>Casablanca</u>?

1. The song is about a train called The City of New Orleans.

2. Many artists and photographers have done funny versions of the painting American Gothic.

3. Tonight Channel 5 is showing two different episodes of Star Trek.

4. Electricity had just arrived in this town the year that Sputnik I was launched.

5. I don't think you spell the name with a k at the end.

6. My parents took these pictures on board the Queen Elizabeth 2.

7. Did you read the interesting editorial in The Des Moines Register last Wednesday?

8. After we read the play Hamlet, we'll see the movie, which is on video.

9. I enjoyed the book Nisei, which is by Bill Hosokawa.

10. The word kvetch, which means to complain, actually comes from Yiddish.

EXERCISE 2 Proofreading Sentences for the Correct Use of Italics

In the sentences below, underline each word or item that should be italicized.

EX. 1. Mom looked in <u>Newsweek</u> to see what's available in entertainment.

1. Friday Night Lights, based on the movie, got good reviews.

2. The book Harry Potter and the Goblet of Fire is as popular as the movie Harry Potter and the Goblet of Fire.

3. A new production of the old opera Xerxes is opening in Santa Fe.

4. The classic book, Jane Eyre, has been made into a movie several times.

5. Mom said that if we don't want to go out, we can stay home and watch re-runs of Good Luck Charlie.

QUOTATION MARKS

12c   **Use quotation marks to enclose a direct quotation—a person's exact words.**

EXAMPLE   "Wait here," said the officer, "until the woman with the flag waves you on."

12d   **A direct quotation begins with a capital letter.**

EXAMPLE   Shane said, "The earlier arrowheads were larger than the later ones."

12e   **When the expression identifying the speaker interrupts a quoted sentence, the second part of the quotation begins with a small letter.**

EXAMPLE   "The clay," said Kelly, "comes from an area near the bottom of the cliffs."

When the second part of a divided quotation is a sentence, it begins with a capital letter.

EXAMPLE   "Look at this," said Mr. Park. "It is a piece of amber."

12f   **A direct quotation is set off from the rest of the sentence by a comma, a question mark, or an exclamation point, but not by a period.**

EXAMPLES   "They will ask for time out," whispered Palani.
              "What good will that do?" asked Jason.
              "We won!" shouted Teresa.

12g   **A period or a comma should always be placed inside the closing quotation marks.**

EXAMPLES   Kwam said, "That's a beautiful serape."
              "My grandmother gave it to me," said Flora.

12h   **A question mark or an exclamation point should be placed inside the closing quotation marks when the quotation itself is a question or an exclamation. Otherwise, it should be placed outside.**

EXAMPLES   "Who has an extra pencil?" I asked. [The quotation is a question.]
              Why did you say, "Space aliens did it"? [The sentence, not the quotation, is a question.]

When both the sentence and a quotation at the end of the sentence are questions (or exclamations), only one question mark (or exclamation point) is used. It is placed inside the closing quotation marks.

EXAMPLE   Did Arthur ask, "Who's in charge here?"

EXERCISE 3 Punctuating Quotations

For each sentence below, insert quotation marks and other marks of punctuation where needed.

EX. 1. **"Who was Daniel Hale Williams?"** asked Marty.

1. Dr. Williams was the doctor said Virgil who founded the first interracial hospital in this country

2. He did more than that explained Lori He also started the first training school for African American nurses

3. What did people do before that asked one student Were they treated at home

4. They were either treated at home said Brian or they were put into dirty wards

5. This doctor even performed heart surgery exclaimed Lina That was unheard of in 1893

EXERCISE 4 Proofreading Sentences for the Use of Quotation Marks

In the sentences below, correctly punctuate and capitalize all direct quotations. If a sentence is correct, write *C* on the line before the sentence.

EX. _____ 1. **"Look out for the cars !"** yelled Karas

_____ 1. We came Ming said to celebrate Kosciuszko Day

_____ 2. Hey, Mark Angelo whispered did you finish your homework

_____ 3. Will you help me asked Lani

_____ 4. What a great way to decorate the invitations exclaimed Gan

_____ 5. You were right she said the store opens at eight o'clock

Using Quotation Marks

On your own paper, create five sentences that each illustrate a rule from this lesson. Then label the sentences with the correct rule number.

EX. 1. *"Did you know," asked Marta, "that I was chosen?"* (*13c*)

12i　When a quotation consists of several sentences, put quotation marks only at the beginning and the end of the whole quotation.

EXAMPLE　　　"Now, you're galloping toward the first barrel. You know you're going to turn and go around it, but the horse doesn't know. So you squeeze with your right knee," said Ron.

12j　When you write dialogue (conversation), begin a new paragraph every time the speaker changes.

EXAMPLE　　　Chad looked nervous as he said, "You guys are not going to believe what I saw last night. Coming home from practice, I saw this thing glowing in the sky, just above the horizon."

"Did you think it was a UFO?" asked Jodie.

"I don't know what it was, but it sure was strange."

"Look," said Umeko, "let's call the state police. They'll know if anyone else reported it."

12k　Use quotation marks to enclose the titles of short works such as short stories, poems, articles, songs, episodes of television programs, and modules and other parts of books.

EXAMPLE　　　Did she sing "Love is the Thing" at the concert?

12l　Use single quotation marks to enclose a quotation within a quotation and to punctuate the title of a short work used within a quotation.

EXAMPLES　　Luana said, "I spoke to the principal, and she said, 'Remember that everyone has the right of free speech.' "

"Have you ever read the poem 'Refugee in America'?" asked Juan.

EXERCISE 5　Punctuating Quotations

In each of the following sentences, insert quotation marks where needed.

EX.　1.　"That poem, called 'Preciosa and the Wind', is by Federico García Lorca," said Ms. Lee.

1.　Who said He who hesitates is lost? asked Ali.

2.　When she walks in said Belinda, we'll sing Happy Birthday.

3.　Before you leave, read the article called The New Youth Brigades.

4.　The first day is the hardest, said Byron. After that you get used to eating less salt.

5.　Did your mother say Patti is always welcome? asked Patti.

6. Kathy handed me the book and said, The funniest module is the one called The Solar Democrat.

7. Is the title of that poem The Silent Crowd?

8. The reviewer said, This book would have been better if it had been shorter. In fact, it might have been wonderful.

9. Did Nikki Giovanni write the poem Knoxville, Tennessee, or did someone else?

10. And then, said Julia, someone started singing The Bear Went Over the Mountain. It was wild!

11. Nathan, Billy asked did you know that there really are dragons in the world?

12. No there aren't countered Nathan.

13. Yes, I read about the Komodo dragon, the forest dragon, and the bearded dragon in the article Amazing Real-life Dragons, answered Nathan.

14. Kiu asked, did Ms. Jeffery say Include material about the Haitian artist Roosevelt in your report?

15. Jerome wants a copy of the brochure Careers in Computers and Electronic Engineering.

EXERCISE 6   Punctuating Paragraphs

On your own paper, rewrite the passage below, adding paragraph breaks and quotation marks where needed.

EX.   [1]   Now listen up! said Ms. Vacca.
    1. *"Now listen up!" said Ms. Vacca.*

[1] Today you will learn something new, said Ms. Vacca. [2] You will learn how to check your spelling with your computer. [3] That's what I need, said Amir. [4] I'm not a really good speller. [5] Ms. Vacca said, This program can help you. [6] However, it won't find certain kinds of mistakes. [7] What kinds won't it find? asked Sopa.

[8] Sometimes, said Ms. Vacca, you can misspell one word by writing another word correctly. [9] You mean, like writing "t-h-e-i-r" instead of "t-h-e-r-e"? asked Amir.

[10] That's exactly what I mean, said Ms. Vacca, and most computers won't catch that kind of mistake.

MODULE 12: PUNCTUATION
APOSTROPHES

The *possessive case* of a noun or a pronoun shows ownership or relationship.

Ownership	Relationship
Toby's poncho	a **night's** sleep
my homework	**dogs'** leashes
everyone's award	**anyone's** guess

12m **To form the possessive case of a singular noun, add an apostrophe and an *s*.**

EXAMPLES the teacher**'s** desk Jess**'s** grades this morning**'s** paper

NOTE A proper noun ending in *s* may take only an apostrophe to form the possessive case if the addition of *'s* would make the name awkward to say.

EXAMPLES Miss Rawlings' book Jesus' teachings Diaz' home

12n **To form the possessive case of a plural noun ending in s, add only the apostrophe.**

EXAMPLES students' names two-days' growth the Stones' home

12o **To form the possessive case of a plural noun that does not end in *s*, add an apostrophe and an *s*.**

EXAMPLES sheep**'s** coats men**'s** barracks teeth**'s** hardness

NOTE Do not use an apostrophe to form the plural of a noun. Remember that the apostrophe shows ownership or relationship.

INCORRECT Two players' have red jerseys.
CORRECT Two **players** have red jerseys
CORRECT The two **players'** jerseys are red.

12p **Do not use an apostrophe with possessive personal pronouns.**

EXAMPLES Is this book **yours?** Is the marker **hers?**

EXERCISE 7   Proofreading for the Use of Apostrophes for Singular Possessives

In the paragraph below, underline each word that needs an apostrophe, and insert the apostrophe. Some sentences have no errors in the use of apostrophes.

EX.   [1] These <u>families'</u> homes were in West Virginia.

[1] The coal miners lives were different from mine. [2] About half of the workers houses had once belonged to the company. [3] Now local families own them. [4] In this community, the mens jobs were basically farming and mining. [5] The womens tasks included factory work, farming, and child care. [6] I visited one mine and was allowed to go down into the mines tunnels. [7] The ones that I visited were about four hundred feet underground. [8] All the miners talk was cheerful until an alarm rang. [9] Everyones face then became serious as we rode to the surface. [10] Although the days work was cut short, no one was hurt.

EXERCISE 8   Writing Possessives

On your own paper, rewrite each of the expressions below by adding an apostrophe to create the correct possessive form.

EX.   1.   the shoes of the dancer
        1.   *the dancer's shoes*

1.   the desk of the boss
2.   the games of the children
3.   the beds of the soldiers
4.   the color of the tooth
5.   the kimono that belongs to somebody

6.   the popcorn of Ms. Thomas
7.   the food of the geese
8.   the chairs of the speakers
9.   the streets of the city
10.   the tortillas of the customer

OTHER USES OF THE APOSTROPHE

A *contraction* is a shortened form of a word, a number, or a group of words.

12q **Use an apostrophe to show where letters, numbers, or words have been omitted (left out) in a contraction.**

Common Contractions	
you are ....you're	they have .... they've
1995................................. '95	she had .... she'd
she will .... she'll	where is .... where's
of the clock .... o'clock	who will .... who'll
I will .... I'll	I would .... I'd

The word *not* can be shortened to *n't* and added to a verb, usually without any change in the spelling of the verb.

EXAMPLES   are not........... are**n't**   could not .... could**n't**
            has not .... has**n't**   should not .... should**n't**
EXCEPTIONS will not .... wo**n't**   cannot .... ca**n't**

Be careful not to confuse contractions with possessive pronouns.

Contractions	Possessive Pronouns
It's late. [**It is**]	**Its** voice was loud.
You're here! [**You are**]	**Your** chili was spicy!
Who's there? [**Who is**]	**Whose** jacket is this?
There's the car. [**There is**]	The red ones are **theirs.**

12r **Use an apostrophe and an *s* to form the plurals of letters, of numerals, and of words referred to as words.**

EXAMPLES   Dot your *i*'**s** and cross your *t*'**s.**
            No, there are two *1*'**s** and two *2*'**s.**
            Try not to begin all sentences with *then*'**s.**

EXERCISE 9   Using Apostrophes Correctly

In the sentences below, underline each word that needs an apostrophe, and insert the apostrophe. On the line before the sentence, write *C* if the sentence is correct.

EX. _____ 1. The boat <u>you're</u> looking at is handmade.

_____ 1. Stay for a while, and well look through the whole museum.

_____ 2. Youll notice that most of the boats are made from animal skins.

_____ 3. Theyre stretched over frames that are made from wood or bone.

_____ 4. The kayak that youre looking at holds just one person.

_____ 5. The bigger boat on your left isnt a kayak, though.

_____ 6. You can tell that boat is an umiak because its hull is much larger.

_____ 7. Some linguists spell *kayak* with *q*s instead of *k*s.

_____ 8. These boats havent been used in many years.

_____ 9. Which of these kayaks was theirs?

_____ 10. Whos talking to your friend about the Inuit hunters?

EXERCISE 10   Writing Contractions

On the line before each sentence below, write a contraction for the italicized word or word pair.

EX. ___*Who's*___ 1. *Who is* that woman?

_____ 1. I *do not* remember her first name, but her last name was Taylor.

_____ 2. I think *it is* a picture of Anna Edson Taylor.

_____ 3. I *cannot* guess why she went over Niagara Falls in a barrel.

_____ 4. *I am* sure she just wanted to prove that it could be done.

_____ 5. I *will not* say if she was brave or if she was foolish.

MODULE REVIEW

A. Proofreading for the Correct Use of Apostrophes, Quotation Marks, and Underlining (Italics)

Rewrite each of the following sentences, using apostrophes, quotation marks, and underlining correctly. [Note: A sentence may contain more than one error.]

EX. 1. The English words their and theyre sound the same, said Inez.

"The English words <u>their</u> and <u>they're</u> sound the same," said Inez.

1. For homework, we are supposed to read the module called Cells in the book called Real Life. _____

_____

2. Whos going to play lead guitar? asked Irina. May I? _____

_____

3. Have you ever, asked Jamal, heard the song called Texas Flood? _____

_____

4. This letter was probably written during the 1800s, said Mr. Koski. It uses words like verily and beshrew. No one writes like that today. _____

_____

_____

5. I love this new jacket! shouted Ms. MacPherson. Lets buy one! _____

_____

6. Was Harry kidding me? asked Selma. Did anyone really write a book called A Wrinkle in Time? _____

_____

_____

7. Some people make their capital qs look like large 2s. _____

_____

8.   Brads parents are going to be pleased because he got an A and two Bs. _____

_____

9.   Theres a picture of the new ocean liner Queen Mary in this volume of the New
      Encyclopaedia Britannica. _____

_____

10.   Sofie asked, Why would anyone even try to say The sixth sheiks sheep
      is sick? _____

_____

11.   The three broadcasters reports did not agree about the game. _____

_____

12.   What do you want to do with yesterdays menus? _____

_____

13.   Two managers employee rules were being discussed. _____

_____

14.   Walt, have you read that article about Miriam Makeba, titled Mama Africa?
      asked Abby. Its about her U.S. tours. _____

_____

15.   Yes, answered Walt. I heard her perform with Paul Simon in 1987. _____

_____

B.   Writing a Dialogue

On your own paper, create a dialogue based on the following old joke. Write the dialogue
in sentence form with direct quotations, and be sure to use quotation marks and other
marks of punctuation correctly. In addition to punctuation marks, you will need to add
dialogue tags to identify who is speaking (*shouted Al; said Earline*).

      Three people were riding on a loud subway. They couldn't hear each other
very well. When Al said it was *windy*, Tranh thought that Al had said
Wednesday. Tranh then remarked that today was Thursday, not Wednesday.
Then Earline spoke up. She thought that Tranh had said *thirsty*, and she
admitted that she was thirsty, too.

      EX.   *"Tranh, it is windy today," shouted Al.*

A dictionary entry is divided into several parts. Study the parts of the sample dictionary entry below.

hap•py (hap'ē), *adj.,* **–pi•er, –pi•est** [Old English *haep*, convenient, suitable] **1.** having a feeling of pleasure [a *happy* person] **2.** giving a feeling of pleasure [a *happy* birthday] **3.** lucky; suitable and fitting [a *happy* chance] **4.** INFORMAL silly or too quick to act [see *slap-happy*] **–hap'pi•ly,** *adv.* **–hap'pi•ness,** *n.* *SYN.* *Happy* suggests "a feeling of pleasure." *Glad* suggests "a reaction of pleasure." *Cheerful* means "showing bright spirits." *Joyful* and *joyous* mean "feeling very happy." *ANT.* sad, melancholy.

1. **Entry word.** The entry word shows the correct spelling of a word. An alternate spelling may also be shown. The entry word shows how the word should be divided into syllables and may also show if the word should be capitalized.

2. **Pronunciation.** The pronunciation is shown using accent marks, phonetic symbols, or diacritical marks. Each *phonetic symbol* represents a specific sound. *Diacritical marks* are special symbols placed above letters to show how those letters sound.

3. **Part-of-speech labels.** These labels are usually abbreviated and show how the entry word should be used in a sentence. Some words may be used as more than one part of speech. In such a case, a part-of-speech label is also given either before or after the set of definitions that matches each label.

4. **Other forms.** Sometimes a dictionary shows spellings of plural forms of nouns, tenses of verbs, or the comparative forms of adjectives and adverbs.

5. **Etymology.** The *etymology* tells how a word (or its parts) entered the English language. The etymology also shows how the word has changed over time.

6.   **Definitions.** If there is more than one meaning, definitions are numbered or lettered.

7.   **Sample of usage.** Some dictionaries include sample phrases to illustrate particular meanings of words.

8.   **Special usage labels.** These labels identify how a word is used (*Slang*), how common a word is (*Rare*), or how a word is used in a special field, such as botany (*Bot.*).

9.   **Related word forms.** These are forms of the entry word created by adding suffixes or prefixes. Sometimes dictionaries also list common phrases in which the word and its related forms appear.

10. **Synonyms and antonyms.** Words similar in meaning are *synonyms*. Words opposite in meaning are *antonyms*. Many dictionaries list synonyms and antonyms at the ends of some word entries.

EXERCISE 1   Using a Dictionary

Use a dictionary to answer the questions below.

EX.   1. How many syllables are in the word *retaliation*? _____*five*_____

1.   How is the word *delirious* divided into syllables? _____

2.   What is the spelling for the plural form of *flamingo*? _____

3.   Give three different meanings for the word *mean.* _____

_____

4.   What is the past tense of *arise*? _____

5.   What is the etymology of the word *maverick*? _____

_____

EXERCISE 2   Writing Words with Alternate Spellings

For each of the words below, write the alternate spelling on the line after the word.

EX.   1. archaeology *archeology*

1.   catalog _____   4.   ameba _____
2.   theater _____   5.   enroll _____
3.   yogurt _____

SPELLING RULES

---

ie and *ei*

13a   **Write *ie* when the sound is long *e*, except after *c*.**

EXAMPLES   chief, believe, piece, relief, receive, deceit
EXCEPTIONS   either, neither, leisure, seize, weird

13b   **Write *ei* when the sound is not long *e*, especially when the sound is long *a*.**

EXAMPLES   weight, height, veil, neighbor, eight, reign
EXCEPTIONS   lie, pie, tie, friend, mischief

EXERCISE 3   Writing Words with *ie* and *ei*

On the line in each word below, write the letters *ie* or *ei* to spell each word correctly. Use a dictionary as needed.

EX. 1. for __*ei*__ gn

1. n _____ ce	6. gr _____ f	11. b _____ ge
2. th _____ r	7. br _____ f	12. c _____ ling
3. f _____ ld	8. sh _____ ld	13. misch _____ f
4. fr _____ ght	9. de _____ ve	14. y _____ ld
5. h _____ r	10. ach _____ ve	15. conc _____ t

–cede, *–ceed*, and *–sede*

13c   **In English, the only word ending in *–sede* is *supersede*. The only words ending in *–ceed* are *exceed*, *proceed*, and *succeed*. All other words with this sound end in *–cede*.**

EXAMPLES   con**cede**, re**cede**, pre**cede**, se**cede**, inter**cede**

EXERCISE 4   Proofreading a Paragraph to Correct Spelling Errors

The following paragraph contains ten spelling errors. Underline the misspelled words. Write the correct spelling above each misspelled word.

preceding
EX.   [1] In the <u>preceeding</u> week, Alexis and I visited the Carnegie Science Center and the aquarium.

[1] The staff of the Carnegie Science Center has succeded in creating a museum that is truly an "amusement park for the mind." [2] The museum has recieved rave reviews from the residents of Pittsburgh. [3] It has also gained worldwide publicity because of its many foriegn visitors. [4] Visitors to the Science Center can liesurely explore four floors of interactive exhibits. [5] After visiting the Science Center, we proceded to the aquarium. [6] Believe me, niether Alexis nor I had ever been to such an exciting aquarium. [7] The giant tank rises to a great hieght. [8] Swimming together in the tank are thousands of fish and many wierd creatures from the deep. [9] The fish seem very freindly and calm, although we did see a brief battle between two barracudas. [10] We also saw a giant tortoise that must have wieghed two hundred pounds.

MODULE 13: SPELLING

PREFIXES AND SUFFIXES

A *prefix* is a letter or a group of letters added to the beginning of a word to change the word's meaning. A *suffix* is a letter or a group of letters added to the end of a word to change its meaning.

13d   When adding a prefix to a word, do not change the spelling of the word itself.

EXAMPLES   mis + spell = **mis**spell   im + possible = **im**possible

over + ripe = **over**ripe   un + rehearsed = **un**rehearsed

13e   When adding the suffix –ness or –ly to a word, do not change the spelling of the word itself.

EXAMPLES   fair + ness = fair**ness**   open + ness = open**ness**

soft + ly = soft**ly**   real + ly = real**ly**

EXCEPTION   For most words that end in *y*, change the *y* to *i* before –*ly* or –*ness*.

EXAMPLES   happy + ness = happ**iness**   busy + ly = bus**ily**

13f   Drop the final silent *e* before a suffix beginning with a vowel.

Vowels are the letters *a, e, i, o, u*, and sometimes *y*. All other letters of the alphabet are *consonants*.

EXAMPLES   gentle + est = gentl**est**   skate + ing = skat**ing**

note + able = not**able**   race + er = rac**er**

EXCEPTION   In words ending in *ce* and *ge*, keep the silent *e* before a suffix beginning with *a* or *o*.

EXAMPLES   notice + able = notic**eable**

courage + ous = courag**eous**

13g   Keep the final *e* before a suffix beginning with a consonant.

EXAMPLES   hope + less = hop**eless**   late + ness = lat**eness**

grace + ful = grac**eful**   sure + ly = sur**ely**

EXCEPTIONS   argue + ment = argu**ment**   true + ly = tru**ly**

EXERCISE 5   Spelling Words with Prefixes and Suffixes

On the line after each partial word equation below, write the word, including the prefix or suffix that is given.

EX.   1.   final + ly   _finaly_

1.   thick + ness   _____
2.   a + rise   _____
3.   un + noticed   _____
4.   cheerful + ly   _____
5.   ir + responsible   _____
6.   return + able   _____
7.   baby + ish   _____
8.   joy + ous   _____
9.   state + ing   _____
10.   outrage + ous   _____

11.   il + legal   _____
12.   up + set   _____
13.   dis + satisfy   _____
14.   im + mortal   _____
15.   easy + ly   _____
16.   anti + toxin   _____
17.   waste + ful   _____
18.   haste + y   _____
19.   en + counter   _____
20.   rake + ed   _____

EXERCISE 6   Spelling Words with Suffixes

On the line after each partial word equation below, write the word, including the suffix that is given.

EX.   1.   ride + ing   _riding_

1.   admire + able   _____
2.   quick + ly   _____
3.   large + est   _____
4.   primary + ly   _____
5.   aviate + or   _____
6.   bossy + ness   _____
7.   rise + ing   _____
8.   peace + able   _____
9.   skate + er   _____
10.   usual + ly   _____

11.   brown + ness   _____
12.   bake + er   _____
13.   joke + ing   _____
14.   argue + ment   _____
15.   nine + ty   _____
16.   range + ing   _____
17.   mighty + ly   _____
18.   change + able   _____
19.   lazy + ly   _____
20.   mis + state   _____

SUFFIXES

13h **For words ending in *y* preceded by a consonant, change the *y* to *i* before any suffix that does not begin with *i*; keep the *y* before a suffix that does begin with *i*.**

EXAMPLES   mystery + ous = myster**ious**   easy + ly = eas**ily**

dry + ing + dr**ying**   hurry + ing = hurr**ying**

EXCEPTIONS   dry + ness = dry**ness**   sly + ly = sl**yly**

13i **Words ending in *y* preceded by a vowel do not change their spelling before a suffix.**

EXAMPLES   boy + hood = bo**yhood**   pray + ed = pra**yed**

EXCEPTIONS   say + ed = sa**id**   day + ly = dai**ly**

13j **Double the final consonant before adding *–ing, –ed, –er,* or *–est* to a one-syllable word that ends in a single consonant preceded by a single vowel.**

EXAMPLES   step + ing = ste**pp**ing   hit + er = hi**tt**er

ship + ed = shi**pp**ed   sad + est = sa**dd**est

With a one-syllable word ending in a single consonant that is not preceded by a single vowel, do not double the consonant before adding *–ing, –ed, –er,* or *–est*.

EXAMPLES   wail + ing = wail**ing**   near + er = near**er**

seem + ed = seem**ed**   cool + est = cool**est**

EXERCISE 7   Spelling Words with Suffixes

On your own paper, write each of the following words, including the suffix that is given.

EX.   1. dim + er

1. *dimmer*

1. crazy + ness	6. stray + ed	11. pay + ing	16. big + est
2. spin + ing	7. drop + ing	12. vary + ous	17. fool + ing
3. wait + ed	8. clear + est	13. play + ed	18. warm + er
4. hot + er	9. worry + ed	14. swim + er	19. try + ing
5. crusty + est	10. hazy + er	15. snap + ed	20. glory + ous

REVIEW EXERCISE

Proofreading to Correct Spelling in a Paragraph

In the paragraph below, underline the twenty spelling errors. Write the correct spelling above each incorrect word.

making

EX.   [1]   Sparky Rucker is <u>makeing</u> history interesting.

[1] Rucker, an African American storyteller from Tennessee, has been delighting audeinces for many years. [2] In his show, which is called *Concieved in Liberty*, he discussed fameous historycal figures and told stories about the culture and music of West Africans who were brought to the United States as slaves. [3] His shows usualy contain many songs; this show included "Amazeing Grace" and "Hambone." [4] Through his work, Rucker has succeded in teaching many people about their African American heritage. [5] In the process, he has truely been making history more real. [6] In many of his shows, he explains the meannings of such slave songs as "Follow the Drinking Gourd." [7] Rucker has sayed that this song was realy a map of the Underground Railroad. [8] Its first line is "Follow the drinking gourd, for the old man is waitting to carry you to Canaan." [9] The drinking gourd is the Big Dipper, and Canaan is Canada, the land where the couragous slaves hopeed to gain their freedom. [10] Storytelling was not unatural in Rucker's family. [11] He remembers his aunts and uncles telling some of the same stories in varyous ways. [12] He often includes hand-clapping rhythms as well. [13] His beleif that no one can easyly separate politics and culture shows in his storytelling.

MODULE 13: SPELLING

PLURALS OF NOUNS

13k **Form the plurals of most nouns by adding –s.**

SINGULAR	shoe	date	desk	donkey	radio	hymn
PLURAL	shoe**s**	date**s**	desk**s**	donkey**s**	radio**s**	hymn**s**

13l **Form the plurals of nouns ending in *s, x, z, ch,* or *sh* by adding –es.**

SINGULAR	glass	tax	waltz	lunch	dish
PLURAL	glass**es**	tax**es**	waltz**es**	lunch**es**	dish**es**

NOTE   Proper nouns usually follow these rules, too.

EXAMPLES   the Espinoza**s**   the Bendex**es**

the Jenkins**es**   the Moskowitz**es**

EXERCISE 8   Spelling the Plurals of Nouns

On the line after each noun, write the correct plural form.

EX.   1.   ax   *axes*

1.   bench   _____

2.   stereo   _____

3.   box   _____

4.   Cortez   _____

5.   wish   _____

6.   class   _____

7.   kiss   _____

8.   rash   _____

9.   grass   _____

10.   nickel   _____

11.   piano   _____

12.   Katz   _____

13.   Delgado   _____

14.   rodeo   _____

15.   area   _____

16.   tray   _____

17.   Vélez   _____

18.   switch   _____

19.   pencil   _____

20.   mask   _____

21.   moth   _____

22.   donkey   _____

23.   fizz   _____

24.   guess   _____

25.   Kirkpatrick   _____

13m   **Form the plurals of nouns ending in _y_ preceded by a consonant by changing the _y_ to _i_ and adding _–es_.**

SINGULAR	story	berry	army	sky	jury
PLURAL	stor**ies**	ber**ries**	arm**ies**	sk**ies**	jur**ies**

EXCEPTION   With proper nouns, simply add _–s_.

      EXAMPLES   the Reilly**s**, the Brodsky**s**

13n   **Form the plurals of nouns ending in _y_ preceded by a vowel by adding _–s_.**

SINGULAR	tray	key	Sunday	boy	play
PLURAL	tray**s**	key**s**	Sunday**s**	boy**s**	play**s**

13o   **Form the plurals of most nouns ending in _f_ by adding _–s_. The plurals of some nouns ending in _f_ or _fe_ are formed by changing the _f_ to _v_ and adding either _–s_ or _–es_.**

SINGULAR	roof	belief	reef	knife	wife	leaf
PLURAL	roof**s**	belief**s**	reef**s**	kni**ves**	wi**ves**	lea**ves**

NOTE   When you are not sure how to spell the plural of a noun ending in _f_ or _fe_, look in a dictionary.

EXERCISE 9   Spelling the Plurals of Nouns

On the line after each noun, write the correct plural form.

EX.   1. baby   _babies_

1. theory _____
2. calf _____
3. bay _____
4. cherry _____
5. life _____
6. valley _____
7. Tuesday _____
8. shelf _____
9. injury _____
10. toy _____

11. gulf _____
12. Sablosky _____
13. honey _____
14. reply _____
15. filly _____
16. thief _____
17. day _____
18. raspberry _____
19. Daly _____
20. scarf _____

13p   **Form the plurals of nouns ending in *o* preceded by a vowel by adding –s. The plurals of many nouns ending in *o* preceded by a consonant are formed by adding –es.**

SINGULAR	stereo zoo	hero	tomato
PLURAL	stereo**s**	zoo**s**	hero**es**	tomato**es**
EXCEPTIONS	tuxedo	tuxedo**s**	hello	hello**s**

Form the plurals of most musical terms ending in *o* by adding –s.

SINGULAR	solo	cello	soprano	contralto
PLURAL	solo**s**	cello**s**	soprano**s**	contralto**s**

NOTE   To form the plurals of some nouns ending in *o* preceded by a consonant, you may add either –s or –es.

SINGULAR	flamingo	grotto	volcano
PLURAL	flamingo**s**	grotto**s**	volcano**s**
	or	*or*	*or*
	flamingo**es**	grotto**es**	volcano**es**

13q   **The plurals of a few nouns are formed in irregular ways.**

SINGULAR	child	man	tooth	goose	mouse
PLURAL	child**ren**	men	teeth	geese	mice

13r   **Form the plural of a compound noun consisting of a noun plus a modifier by making the modified noun plural.**

SINGULAR	sister-in-law	man-of-war	stock market
PLURAL	sister**s**-in-law	men-of-war	stock market**s**

EXERCISE 10   Spelling the Plurals of Nouns

On the line after each noun, write the correct plural form.

EX.   1.   radio   *radios*

1. veto _____
2. gaucho _____
3. woman _____
4. studio _____
5. father-in-law _____

6. blue jay _____
7. foot _____
8. baby sitter _____
9. potato _____
10. video _____

EXERCISE 11 Proofreading to Correct Spelling in a Paragraph

In the paragraph below, underline the fifteen errors in spelling. Write the correct spelling above each misspelled word.

children
EX. [1] All of the <u>childs</u> in the international chorus visited our school.

[1] Because they have naturally high voices, most of the singers are sopranoes, and only a few are altoes. [2] During the concert, echos of soaring voices, almost like those of Baltimore oriolees or other singing birds, filled the hall. [3] The singers were accompanied by two womans who played grand pianoes and two mans who played piccoloes. [4] Afterwards, the singers met with members of our school chorus to tour our practice studioes. [5] Then we all had lunch on the patioes, which were only a few foots away from the music wing and the art department. [6] Two mans from a television station interviewed the singers and taped videoes for tonight's news broadcast. [7] Two radio stations are planning to play excerptes from the concert on separate broadcasts next week. [8] Tonight, several members of the chorus will sing soloes during the City Symphony's performance.

EXERCISE 12 Using Plurals Correctly

On your own paper, write a sentence, using the plural form of each word below.

EX. 1. foot
     1. *Please wear shoes to protect your feet.*

1. hobo   3. great-uncle   5. cargo   7. rodeo   9. mosquito
2. ox   4. banjo   6. maid of honor 8. lingo   10. Congo snake

A. Correcting Spelling Errors in Sentences

Underline all misspelled words in each sentence below. Then write each misspelled word correctly in the space above the word.

> *brief*
> EX. 1. Tamara and Louis had a <u>breif</u> meeting to discuss the film.

1. My nieghbor, Takara Asano, is a foriegn exchange student from Japan.

2. Two soloes by a famous opera singer will preceed tonight's concert.

3. I know she will easily succede as leader of the altoes.

4. I was disatisfied with the overipe fruit.

5. Suddenly the two children burst into an outragous arguement.

6. We bought plentyful supplyes before the storm.

7. Dentists usualy offer new teethbrush to their patients after yearly checkups.

8. The Sanchezs will spend a liesure weekend in Galveston.

9. The factories are shiping the stereoes in heavy boxes to avoid damage.

10. Our ponys wear colorful harnesses when pulling the sRleghs.

11. The receeding floodwaters had ruined the crops in the feilds.

12. I admire my freind's openess.

13. Were you planing to make such a gracful entrance?

14. The spot on the carpet is realy noticable!

15. The store recieved ninty hatboxes today.

16. How many flys ball did you catch in the outfeild today?

17. After traceing the vase's outline, Melba easly added the color.

18. The men carriing the bags were my shipsmate.

19. The students wanted to meet all of thier facultys sponsor.

20. The flock of wild geeses flying above us was a beautyful sight.

B.   Proofreading a Paragraph to Correct Spelling Errors

The paragraph below contains twenty spelling errors. Underline each misspelled word, and write the correct spelling above it.

reefs

EX.   [1]   Diver Michael Grofik found a treasure in the <u>reeves</u> off the Florida coast.

[1] Grofik was one of the memberes of a team sent to the Florida waters by a

company nameed Historical Research & Development, Inc. [2] He and his freinds and

partners were diveing about one hundred yards off the coast of Sebastian, Florida, in

eight foots of water. [3] When the other mans and womans on the team took their

dayly break to eat their lunchs, Grofik did not. [4] He decided that continueing his

searchs for treasure might be more rewarding than stoping for lunch. [5] That decision

luckyly payed off; in fact, it exceded even Grofik's bigest dreams and expectationes.

[6] He found many peices of gold jewelry, which historyans beleive came from a

Spanish ship that sank off the Florida coast in 1715!

C.   Identifying Correctly Spelled Words

For each of the following items, underline the correctly spelled word in parentheses.

EX.   1. a (<u>*brief,*</u> *brief*) vacation

1.   a (*belief, belief*) in children
2.   the (*weight, wieght*) of the package
3.   a painted (*ceiling, cieling*)
4.   a (*mispelled, misspelled*) word
5.   many (*skaters, skatters*)
6.   a silly (*argument, arguement*)
7.   an (*immpossible, impossible*) dream
8.   (*skateing, skating*) on the pond
9.   a (*changeable, changable*) nature
10.   (*drying, driing*) the towels
11.   an (*unatural, unnatural*) appearance

12. two new (*radioes, radios*)

13. serving mashed (*potatos, potatoes*)

14. living near the (*Kirkes, Kirks*)

15. washing the (*knives, knifes*)

16. (*trays, trayes*) for the salad

17. three (*sopranoes, sopranos*)

18. eight (*geese, gooses*)

19. several (*man-of-war, men-of-war*)

20. (*their, thier*) new home

D. Writing a Language Workshop Lesson

You are a student intern who has been asked by the United Nations to travel to another country. Your assignment is to run a spelling workshop for students who are learning English as a second language. Select five spelling rules from this module to present in your first class. On the lines following these instructions, write each rule. Then provide examples. Finally, for each rule, create five exercise items to give to the students to check their understanding of the rule. For each exercise, create a list of answers on a separate piece of paper.

EX. 1. *RULE: To form plurals of nouns ending in s, x, z, ch, or sh, you must add –es.*

EXAMPLES: glass, glasses; box, boxes; waltz, waltzes; beach, beaches; wish, wishes

EXERCISE ITEM: 1. fox 1. foxes

_____

_____

_____

_____

_____

_____

_____

_____

_____

300 Spelling Words (continued)

official	practically
omit	precede
operation	precisely
opportunity	preferred
oppose	prejudice
optimism	preparation
orchestra	pressure
organization	primitive
originally	privilege
paid	probably
paradise	procedure
parallel	proceed
particularly	professor
peasant	proportion
peculiar	psychology
percentage	publicity
performance	pursuit
personal	qualities
personality	quantities
perspiration	readily
persuade	reasonably
petition	receipt
philosopher	recognize
picnic	recommendation
planning	referring
pleasant	regretting
policies	reign
politician	relieve
possess	remembrance
possibility	removal

300 Spelling Words (continued)

renewal	sponsor
repetition	straighten
representative	substantial
requirement	substitute
residence	subtle
resistance	succeed
responsibility	successful
restaurant	sufficient
rhythm	summary
ridiculous	superior
sacrifice	suppress
satire	surprise
satisfied	survey
scarcely	suspense
scheme	suspicion
scholarship	temperament
scissors	tendency
senate	thorough
sensibility	transferring
separate	tremendous
sergeant	truly
several	unanimous
shepherd	unfortunately
sheriff	unnecessary
similar	urgent
skis	useful
solemn	using
sophomore	vacancies
source	vacuum
specific	varies

COMMONLY MISSPELLED WORDS

The following list contains seventy-five words that are often misspelled. To find out which words give you difficulty, ask someone to read you the list in groups of twenty-five. Write down each word; then check your spelling. Make a list in your spelling notebook of any word you misspelled. Keep reviewing your list until you have mastered the correct spelling.

75 Commonly Misspelled Words		
ache	forty	speak
across	friend	speech
again	grammar	straight
all right	guess	sugar
almost	half	surely
always	having	tear
answer	heard	though
belief	hour	through
built	instead	tired
business	knew	together
busy	know	tomorrow
buy	laid	tonight
can't	likely	tough
color	making	trouble
coming	meant	truly
cough	minute	Tuesday
could	often	until
country	once	wear
doctor	ready	Wednesday
doesn't	really	where
don't	safety	which
eager	said	whole
easy	says	women
every	shoes	won't
February	since	Write

SPELLING WORDS

Learn to spell the following words if you don't already know how. They're grouped so that you can study them ten at a time.

300 Spelling Words	
absence	authority
absolutely	available
acceptance	basically
accidentally	beginning
accommodate	believe
accompany	benefit
accomplish	benefited
accurate	boundary
accustomed	calendar
achievement	campaign
acquaintance	capital
actually	category
administration	certificate
affectionate	characteristic
agriculture	chief
amateur	circuit
ambassador	circumstance
analysis	civilization
analyze	column
announcement	commissioner
anticipate	committee
apology	comparison
apparent	competent
appearance	competition
approach	conceivable
approval	conception
arguing	confidential
argument	conscience
assurance	conscious
attendance	consistency

300 Spelling Words (continued)	
constitution	embarrass
continuous	emergency
control	employee
cooperate	encouraging
corporation	environment
correspondence	equipped
criticism	essential
criticize	evidently
cylinder	exaggerate
debtor	exceedingly
decision	excellent
definite	excessive
definition	excitable
deny	exercise
description	existence
despise	expense
diameter	extraordinary
disappearance	fascinating
disappointment	fatal
discipline	favorably
disgusted	fictitious
distinction	financier
distinguished	flourish
dominant	fraternity
duplicate	frequent
economic	further
efficiency	glimpse
eighth	glorious
elaborate	grabbed
eligible	gracious

300 Spelling Words (continued)

graduating	knowledge
grammar	leisure
gross	lengthen
gymnasium	lieutenant
happiness	likelihood
hasten	liveliness
heavily	loneliness
hindrance	magazine
humorous	maneuver
hungrily	marriage
hypocrisy	marvelous
hypocrite	mechanical
icy	medieval
ignorance	merchandise
imagination	minimum
immediately	mortgage
immense	multitude
incidentally	muscle
indicate	mutual
indispensable	narrative
inevitable	naturally
innocence	necessary
inquiry	negligible
insurance	niece
intelligence	noticeable
interfere	obligation
interpretation	obstacle
interrupt	occasionally
investigation	occurrence
judgment	offense